REAL IRISH FAIRIES OF DONEGAL

J.A. GREENLEAF

SWORDPOINT INTERCONTINENTAL, LTD.

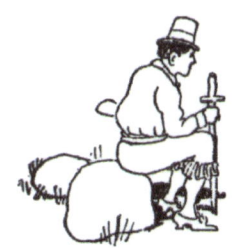

Cataloging in Publication Data is available
from the Library of Congress.

ISBN: 615465706
ISBN-13: 978-0615465708

Published by:
Swordpoint Intercontinental, Ltd.
7202 Giles Road, Suite 4212
La Vista, Nebraska 68128 USA

ALSO BY J.A. GREENLEAF

Donegal Fairy Stories
by
Seumas MacManus
Edited by
Joseph A. Greenleaf

Sudden Light
by
J.A. Greenleaf

DEDICATION

This book is lovingly dedicated to my bride of many years, Karlene, to my sons, Joseph and Jacob, and in memory of my son, Benjamin.

REAL IRISH FAIRIES OF DONEGAL

CONTENTS

1 MALIN HEAD

Ireland, the land of "saints and scholars"—and fairies.

As an old Irish woman said, "I don't believe in fairies, but that doesn't mean they don't exist!"

I believe in fairies—I always have—I just had never seen any. But, then again, I'd never seen either the Antarctic or the Planet Neptune, but I still believe they exist—and the many pic-

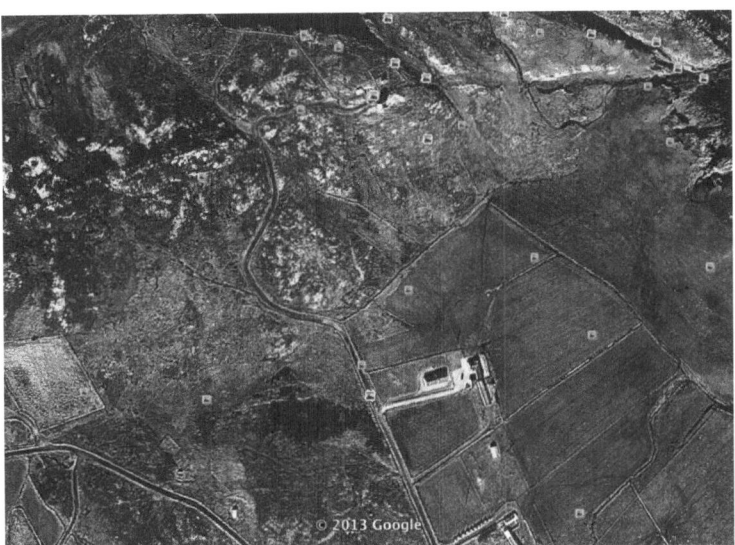

tures of them weren't "doctored" in some way!

Most Americans think of fairies as something like Tinker Bell, a figure on a box of Lucky Charms cereal, or out of the old Sean Connery movie, "Darby O'Gill and the Little People."

In Ireland, there's a great deal more healthy respect for the "wee folk." Standing stone circles, erected around the time the Egyptians built the pyramids, are often called "fairy circles." Many Irish people will demure when invited to visit them, and, if they do, they will usually refuse to enter into the ring, for fear of offending the fairies.

Unlike the Disney creations, Irish fairies can be mean, vengeful and dangerous; cross them at your peril. Stories of changelings—children and others who were transformed by the fairy folk into someone who looked like the original person, but who was, in fact, someone or something else. The cry of the Banshee in the night often portended someone's death. Stories are still told of modern roads under construction that had to be diverted—at considerable expense—to avoid having to cut down a "fairy bush"—a certain blackthorn bush. To cut down the fairy bush would be to invite certain doom.

If you bring up the subject of fairies in Ireland, there's usually someone who has a relative—usually a grandmother—who has a leprechaun or some other kind of "fairy folk" in their "back garden," or as Americans would say, their "backyard."

When my book, *Donegal Fairy Stories* first came out, a young woman I worked with in Donegal told me about her own grandmother, or "gran" who, after looking out the garden window of her house in Inishowen, County Donegal, saw a tiny man wearing a red suit and hat, who, when he saw her, dashed across the garden. Her gran went after him, and saw him jump onto a low, stone wall and over to the far side. When Gran got there, the wee man was gone and there was nothing but an open field.

Left, my house, "Solas Tobann," ("Sudden Light"), from space. Banba's Crown and tower beyond. Copyright © 2013 Google. Image Copyright © 2013 DigitalGlobe.

It is easy to act the "suave sophisticate," and say, smugly, that there is a simple explanation for every one of the stories, that they are either simple fiction, "tall tales," senility, delusions or the fruits of an overactive imagination. And, quite possibly, in many cases, could well be true. But, I ask you, can every single instance be dismissed, out-of-hand? As Sigmund Freud once said, "Sometimes, a cigar is a cigar."

Our house in Ireland is a single story "bungalow." Since there are no ranch houses called that in Ireland, it is a bungalow, which is, simply, a one-story detached house. In Ireland, houses stand alone—a "detached house," some are "semi-detached houses," (what American would call a "duplex") or are terrace homes—in America, a row house.

There has always been another bungalow nearby, perhaps one hundred yards from our house, lying perpendicular to ours, one which is two hundred or more years old, and has been used only occasionally since we've been there—a "holiday home." Next to it, in the past year or so, what was once its old barn, was demolished and a new bungalow, also perpendicular to our house, was built in its place. Other than these three houses, there are no other houses very close. The photograph of me shows Banba's

Lagg Church, near Trawbreaga Bay

Crown in the distance, with the Tower above it. Our house is beyond the houses shown in the photograph, and is just at the foot of Banba's Crown hill. I am standing in the road at the edge of Ballyhillion.

Malin Head is the headlands of the Inishowen Peninsula. "Inishowen" means "Owen's Island." Owen was one of the sons of Niall of the Nine Hostages, and lived hundreds and hundreds of years ago.

During Owen's time, Inishowen was, in fact, an island, or, in fact, several islands.

Inishowen is an uncommonly beautiful peninsula, hard on the western edge of Northern Ireland and, in fact, at least as far as Malin Head is concerned, is farther north than the most northerly point of Northern Ireland. Nicknamed "Ireland

in miniature," Inishowen looks a lot like the island of Ireland, with inlets, lakes, mountains and glens. Many thatched houses are still in daily use and a common "traffic jam" in Inishowen is farmers—male and female—herding cows, sheep or horses down the lane, from one field to another.

Several hundred years ago, the waters of the North Atlantic were higher, and there was a waterway at the foot of the peninsula, making it an island, as was Inch Island to its west, at the foot of Lough Swilly. To the west of Inishowen is Lough Foyle and the Atlantic Ocean. While both the Swilly and the Foyle are called "lough," (the Irish word for "lake," like "loch" [as in Loch Ness] in Scots Gaelic, and pronounced as "lock" in English) neither is a lake, but rather, are fjords, since they both open to the sea.

Today, you drive over a lovely seventeenth-century arched stone bridge into Malin Town, over a finger of Trawbreaga Bay (which, according to legend, holds the underwater castle of a Fairy King and Queen). In days gone by, the Bay went from Lough Swilly to the west to the Atlantic on the east.

Malin Head itself was also an island. Today, you can drive all the way to the top of Malin Head, to Banba's Crown, named after one of the three mythical queens of Ireland.

Atop Banba's Crown is a small castle-appearing structure which was built around 1802 as a signal tower for the British Royal Navy, ever on the lookout for Napoleon's Navy, which, faced with a half-pay junior officer and a few "other ranks" (enlisted men), wisely kept away.

In the latter part of the 1800s, the tower passed to Lloyd's of London—the ship insurers—who watched for ships passing by Malin Head after a long ocean crossing. Sighting the ship meant that it would likely safely make port in England, and the insurers' syndicate could breathe easier.

During the First and Second World Wars, lookouts manned concrete lookout posts, first the British Army and then, in World War Two (or "The Emergency" as it was called in Ireland), the Irish Army watched for ships and, later, airplanes.

Stones painted white spelled out the word, "Éire," (pronounced, "Air-ah") the Irish-language word for "Ireland," announcing to belligerents on both sides that they were now over neutral Ireland. The stones remain.

There is the site of an ancient Stone Age village on one of the rocky outcrops below the tower and, a short walk away is a deep fissure in the stone called "Hell's Hole," where the ocean crashes in.

A natural stone arch and a sea cave are nearby, and, on a fair day, you can see the islands of Scotland in the distance. Closer in is the desert island of Inishtrahull, upon which is a modern, automated lighthouse and the remains of an ancient lighthouse, hundreds of years old.

Farther way is the "Wee House of Malin," which is actually a cave where Catholic Mass was heard in secret during the years that Catholicism was

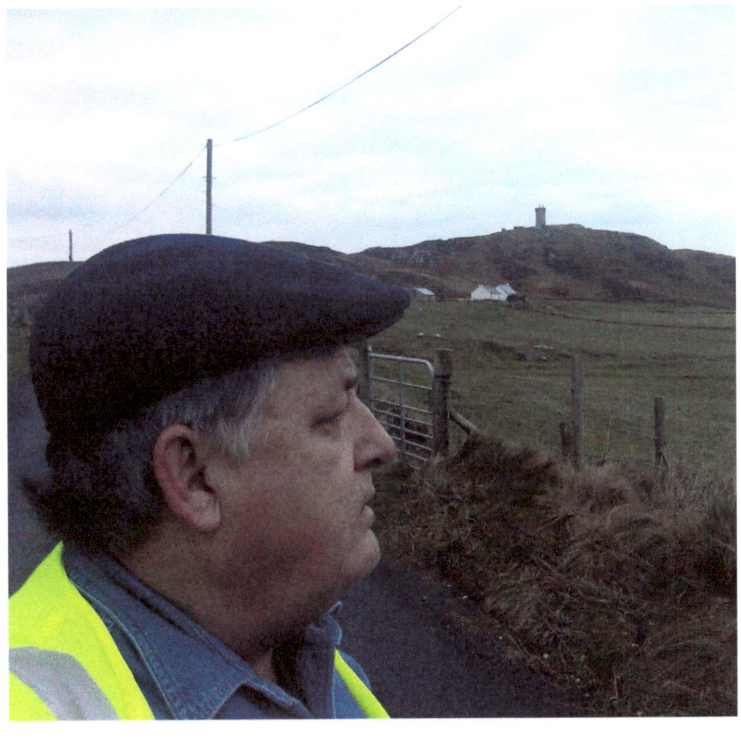

J.A. Greenleaf, the author

repressed by the English. Next to it are the ruins of a stone church and the reputed burial place of its hermit monk resident.

The nearby beach is a "raised beach," consisting of countless rounded stones some of which are semi-precious, dropped there by the retreated glacier.

Below, Karlene Greenleaf, with her hand in a modern standing stone, on the scenic overlook above Trawbreaga Bay, on a windy day.

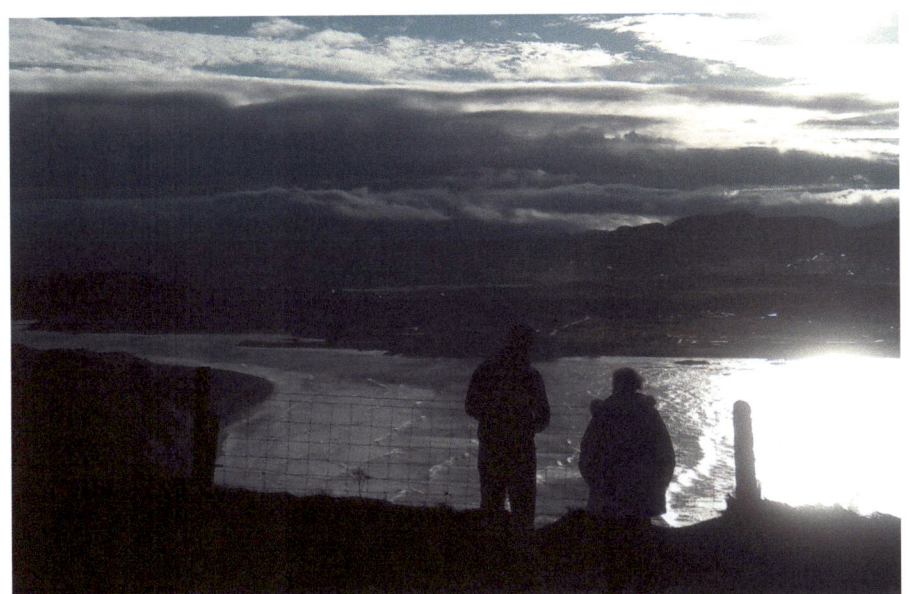

Trawbreaga Bay. Karlene Greenleaf on the right.

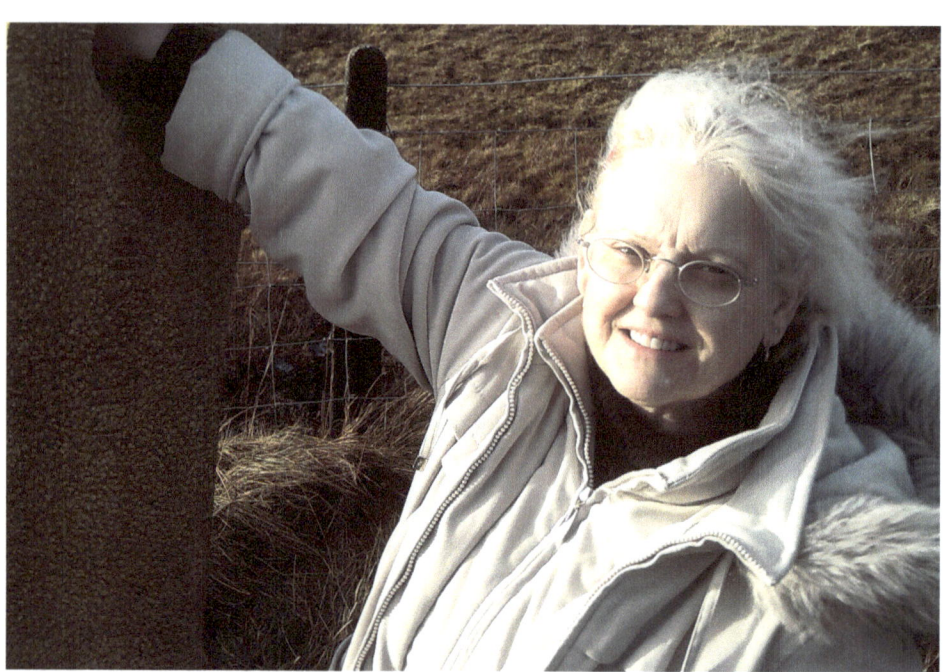

2 THE FAIRIES

On June 21, 2003, I was at the house by myself, alone with just my Kerry Blue Terrier dog, "Murphy."

It being nice weather, sometime after 11:00 o'clock at night, I decided to go outside with Murphy to look at the stars. Unpolluted by lights from any civilization, a panoply of stars could be seen on a nice night, as it was. The only lights were those from the house windows and two halogen outside lights near each of the two doors. They were both lit, being automatic.

Murph *(below)* and I went outside through the

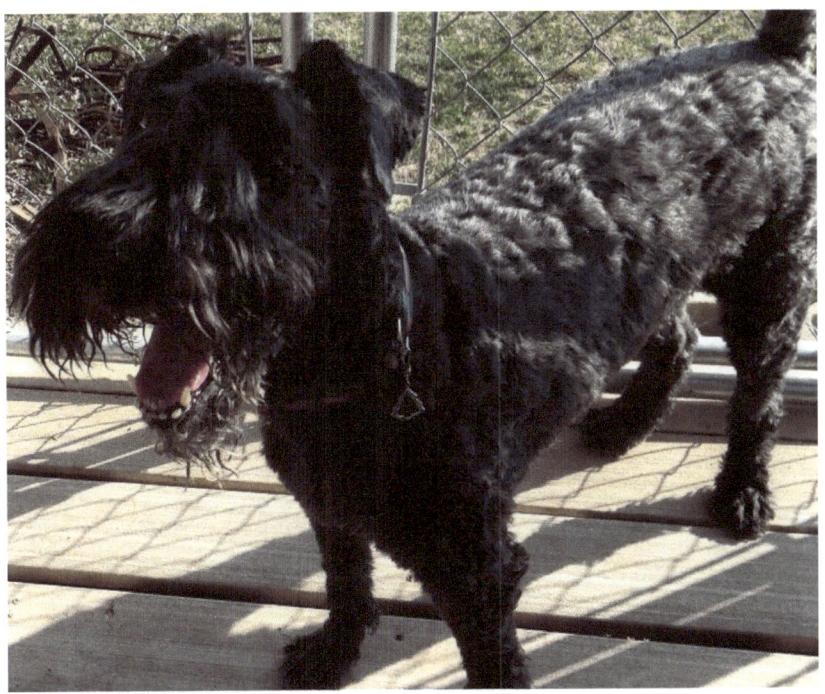

door from the laundry room, the door farthest from the road, and walked down the drive, towards the road.

In the light of the outside lights, I spotted a large number—perhaps as many as thirty—good-sized creatures with white wings, on the grass between the driveway and the wooden fence. The photo-graph of the verge shows what it looks like in the Winter of 2013, in January, overgrown grass and all. The whirligig is long gone.

Murphy paid them no heed, and they ignored him as well.

I came abreast of the creatures, perhaps eighteen inches away from them, on the ground, and, as one, they all flew off the ground and flew towards me, as I stood, transfixed.

They rose to my eye level and began to fly in a circle, counterclockwise (or, "anti-clockwise," as they say in Ireland). They made a loud "clacking" sound, but how they made it, I had no idea.

They looked like insects of some kind, but they were quite large—almost the size of my hand. Each of them had a flesh-colored body, blond hair, flesh-colored legs, and a insect-like thorax circled with multiple lavender bands.

I briefly thought of putting out my hand, but I had no idea whether I would be bitten or not. Murphy simply stood by my side, watching them with me.

After a moment, they all flew, together, back to the ground and formed into semi-circles on the grass.

A short time before, I had purchased a Canon digital camera. It had an optical viewfinder as well as an LCD screen, but I hadn't completely explored how to see images in the LCD screen.

I went into the house through the front door and got the camera from one of the rooms. I was convinced that it was probably a waste of time, as I was sure they had gone to wherever it was they had come from. I certainly had no idea where that might be, as I had not seen anything like them in the five or so years I'd lived there at that point.

With Murphy trotting behind me, I went back outside. Most of them had left, but there were still some on the grass..

As I raised the camera to my eye, I realized I couldn't see a blessed thing through the optical viewfinder and I did not know how to use the LCD screen. I felt I had nothing to lose, so I just pointed the camera in their general direction

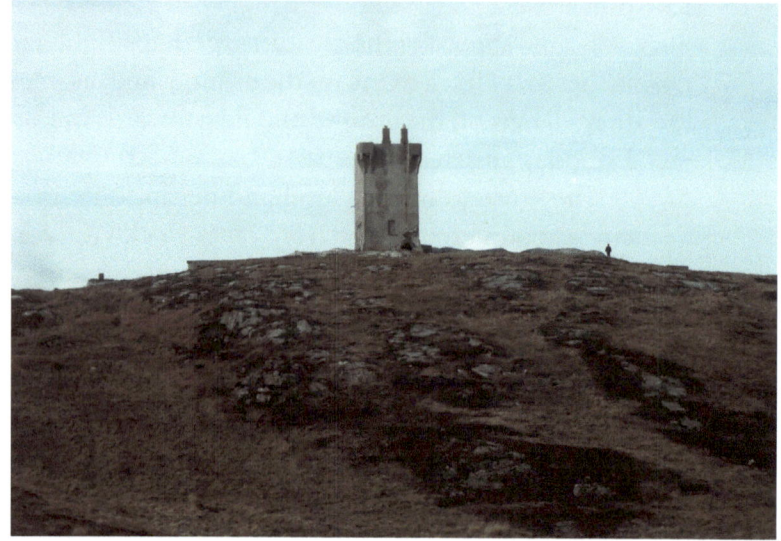

Left, the Tower atop Banba's Crown hill, behind our house at Malin Head.

and fired off five flash photographs, each a few moments apart.

I simply hoped for the best, but fully expected that, either the camera would be aimed at bare grass or, if it were pointed in their direction, they would not appear in the photographs—sort of like taking pictures, it is said, of ghosts—nothing appears in the pictures.

I considered the possibility that I was imagining all of this or was, somehow, dreaming it.

The photographs were there, however, and I wasn't dreaming it.

Below, Glasheedy Island, at the mouth of Trawbreaga Bay, from the scenic overlook at Lagg Dunes.

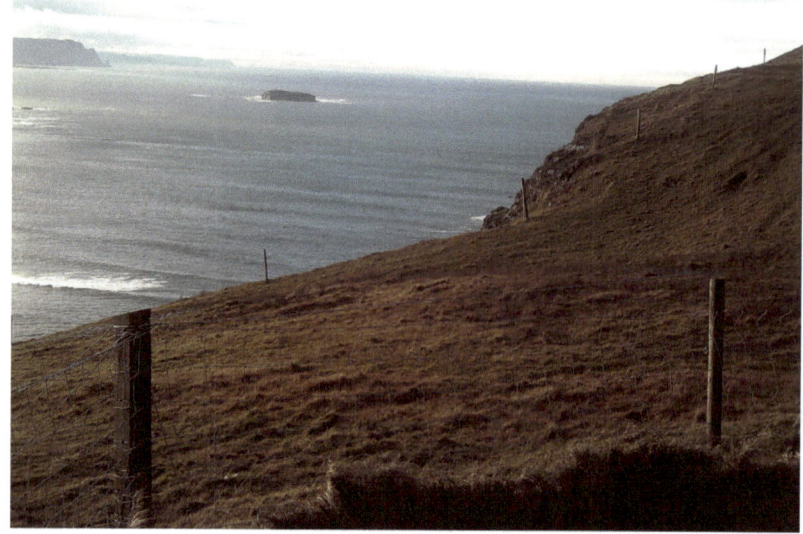

3 PHOTOGRAPHS

It was nearing midnight when I heard the telephone ring inside the house, so Murphy and I went back inside. I didn't see what the creatures

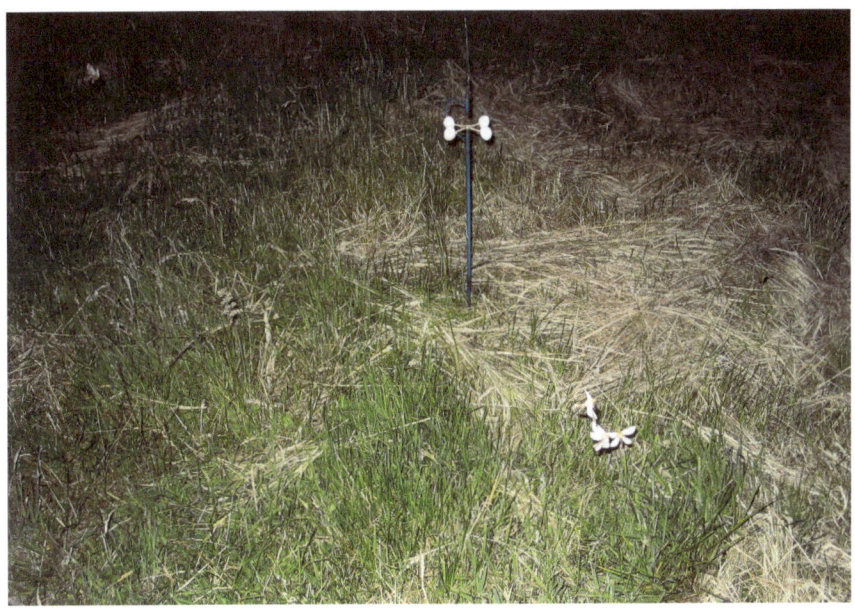

did when I left.

Ringing me was my sister, Patricia Milligan, who lived north of Letterkenny, about fifty miles away.

"What are you doing?" she asked.

"I was out in the front garden, taking pictures of fairies."

"Sure you were. Have you been drinking?"

"No," I reassured her. "I will send you pictures by e-mail, if they turned out."

"If they turn out…" she laughed.

A few moments later, I had extracted five pictures from the memory card of the cam-

era and, to my amazement and utter delight, there they were, on four of the five photographs. The fifth seemed to be just grass, some of the rail fence and a little whirligig I had in the grass.

I sent them to her and she called me back.

"I guess you really *were* taking pictures of fairies!"

I related what had happened, and she was completely amazed.

The next morning, she phoned me again and said, "Do you know what yesterday was?"

I said I didn't at the time, but that morning, before she called, I realized that it was the Vernal Equinox: a magical time when wondrous things happened.

She asked if I was going to publicize the photographs. I said I didn't want to end up on the cover of "The News of the World." Besides, I was working for the American Air Force and I had a security clearance. If I came out with a story about seeing "wee folk" and fairies, I might lose both my security clearance and my job. Besides, who would hire a lawyer who saw fairies?

And so, time went by. "The News of the World" went out of business (probably from not publishing

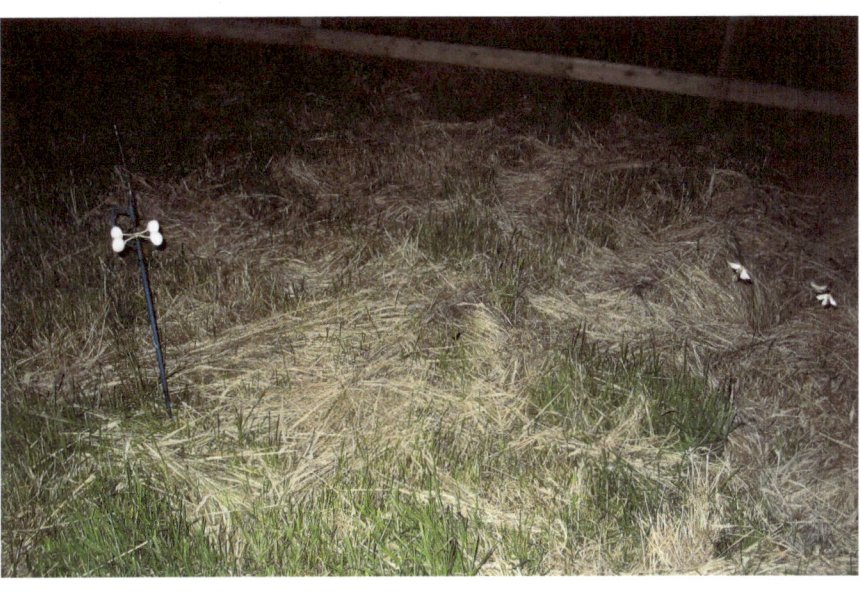

enough fairy pictures), I retired from the service of the Air Force and began writing.

I have shown the pictures to a select few people, most of whom were thunderstruck and uniformly urged me to publish them. Some, like our friend and physician, Síofra, (whose name means "fairy" in Irish) said, "I believe in fairies, but I think you faked these pictures, just like my husband would." I assured her I didn't, but, to no avail.

Patricia showed them to several old ladies in Donegal and they flatly declared them to be real Donegal fairies. They said they had lived all of their 70 or 80 years in Donegal and never have they seen anything like them.

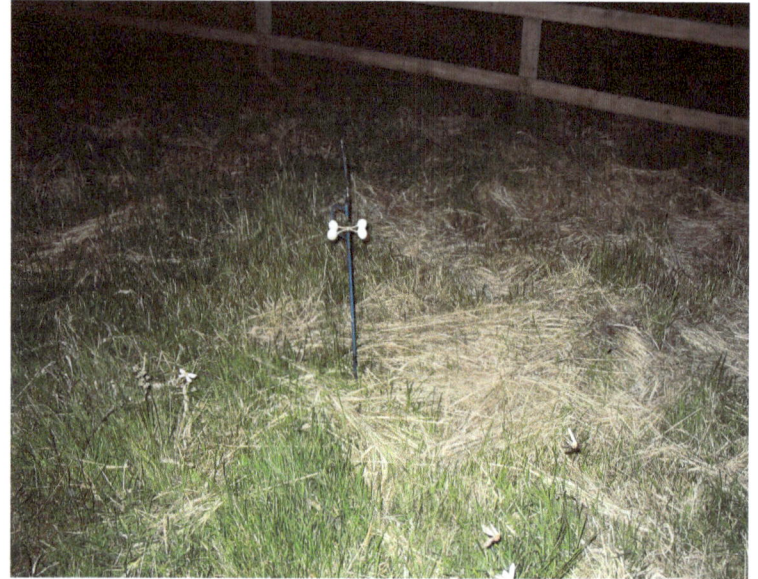

Right, three fairies on the right of the photograph, one to the left of the whirligig.

Below, one figure, thought to be a leprechaun, or another fairy, to the left of the cup anemometers of the whirligig.

Below, right, one fairy, clearly showing a blond head.

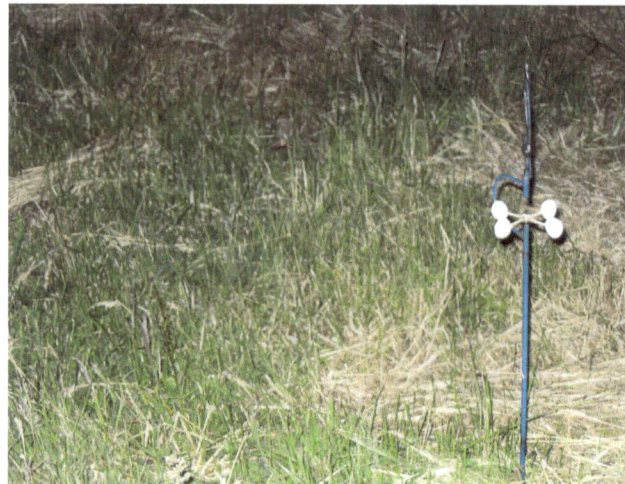

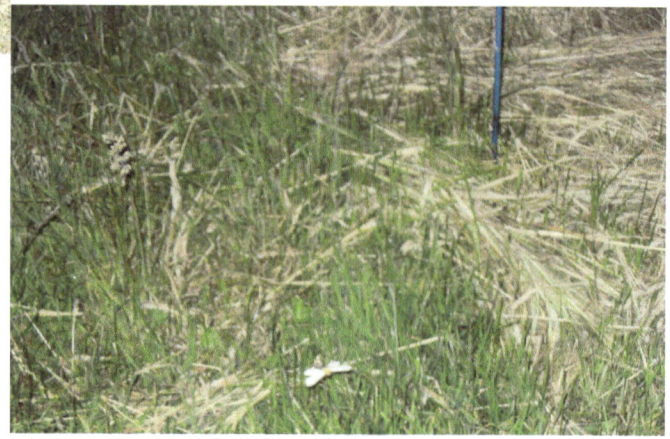

4 WHAT ARE THEY?

I researched various books in the library and online, and could see nothing like them, including in a huge, thick book of butterflies and moths of England and Ireland. None even came close.

An entomologist—a bug doctor—who was a professor of entomology in Dublin was visiting my house. He looked at the photographs and declared that he had no idea what they were. He probably though the photographs were the result of "Photoshopping" or some kind of chicanery, but was too polite to say so.

Right, front of our house. Below, grassy verge, present day, in front of the house with the sea beyond.

And so, the photographs have languished—until now.

Although I absolutely guarantee and swear that they are photographs that I took in 2003 in Malin Head, and that they have not been altered or faked in any way whatsoever, I am just as certain that, the moment this book is published—or even beforehand—that various people will come forth and say they can "prove" the pictures were faked, because of thus-and-so, here-and-how and

the like. If it makes them happy to do so, work away. I know they are real and completely genuine. Any expert is welcome to examine the digital copies and perform any tests that they like.

That being said, I cannot state with any certainty that they aren't some kind of obscure insect. They look like insects, albeit none I have ever seen before: they have wings, insect-like legs and a tapered thorax, just like many moths and butterflies.

Many things about them, however, are very much unlike any insects I have ever seen:

- They were not attracted to the bright halo-

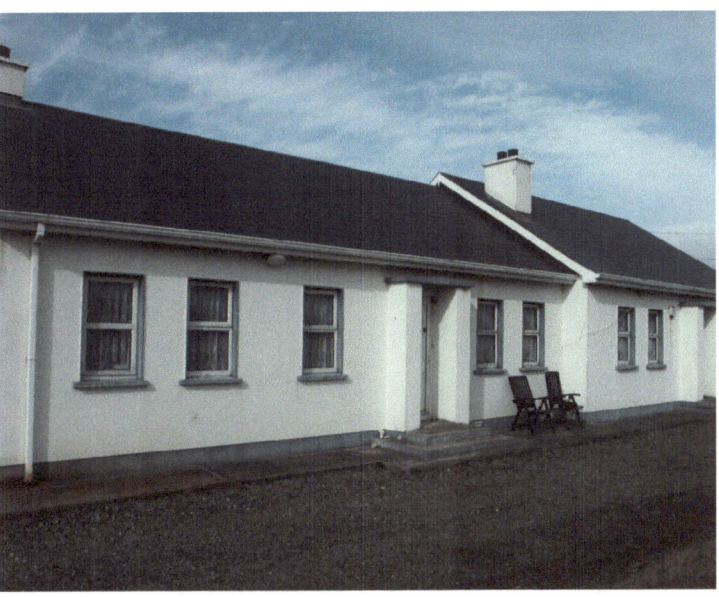

gen house lights, or the window lights.
- They were neither afraid of me nor my dog.
- They had been in a semi-circle.
  - They flew up as if to greet me, or, at least, to inspect me.
  - They made a loud, "clacking" sound, unlike anything I had ever heard before, or read of.
  - They didn't try to land on me or otherwise hurt me.
  - They had yellow hair.
  - They had flesh-colored bodies and legs.
  - They had lavender rings around their thoraxes.

As I said, four of the photographs show the fairies. The fifth appeared

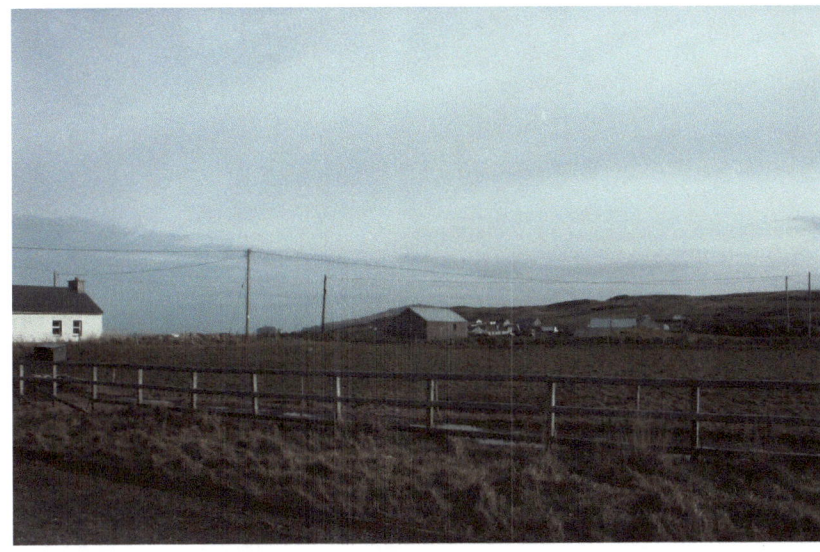

to only show grass, the fence and the whirligig. I was mistaken. I closely examined each section of all of the photographs, including the fifth, "empty" one. Zooming in as far as practical, in searching to the left of the whirligig, there, in the grass was what

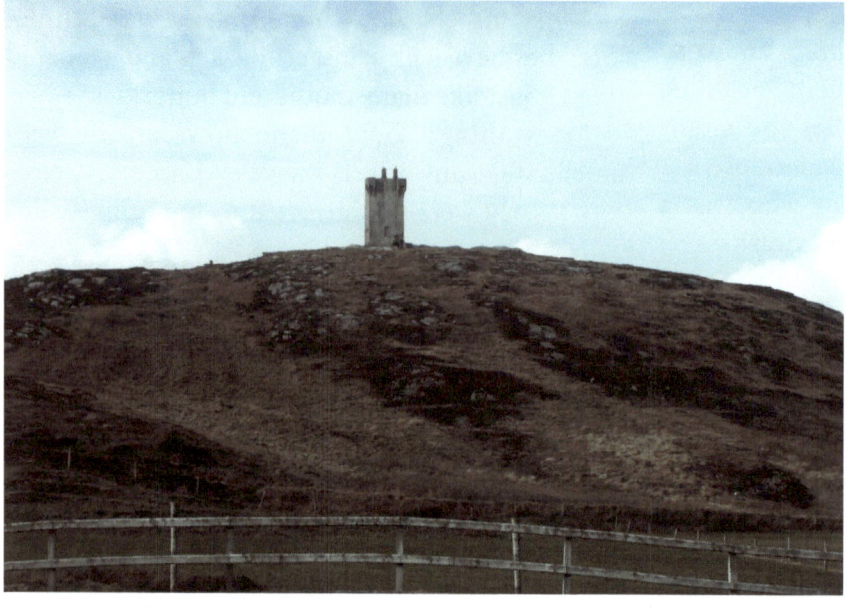

stories about leprechauns with wings, but who can say? You can judge for yourself.

I believe that the ones with white wings are fairies and they are what the old people saw in ancient times and similarly concluded that they were fairies.

Where they came from, at least at my house, and where they went, is a mystery. I'm sure they didn't travel far, and probably live underground. They might hibernate for years at a time; I just don't know.

Left, Banba's Crown and the Tower, with my fence in the foreground.

I first thought was another fairy. This one, however, while it had four wings, the wings were more transparent than the fairies' opaque, white, wings. It appeared to be looking straight at me, with its wings to each side. It had what appears to be two large eyes. Atop its head was either a tall, green, hat or a large blade of grass directly behind its head. It looks more like a hat to me, or even a hat made from grass!

It is obvious that this lone creature is very different from the others. It could be a different type of fairy, or something else altogether. I think it is what people have always believed were leprechauns. Granted, I have never heard any

Below, our house, left, the modern bungalow in the center, and the old cottage to the right. The fairies appeared just about in front of my house's left front door. Banba's Crown to the rear.

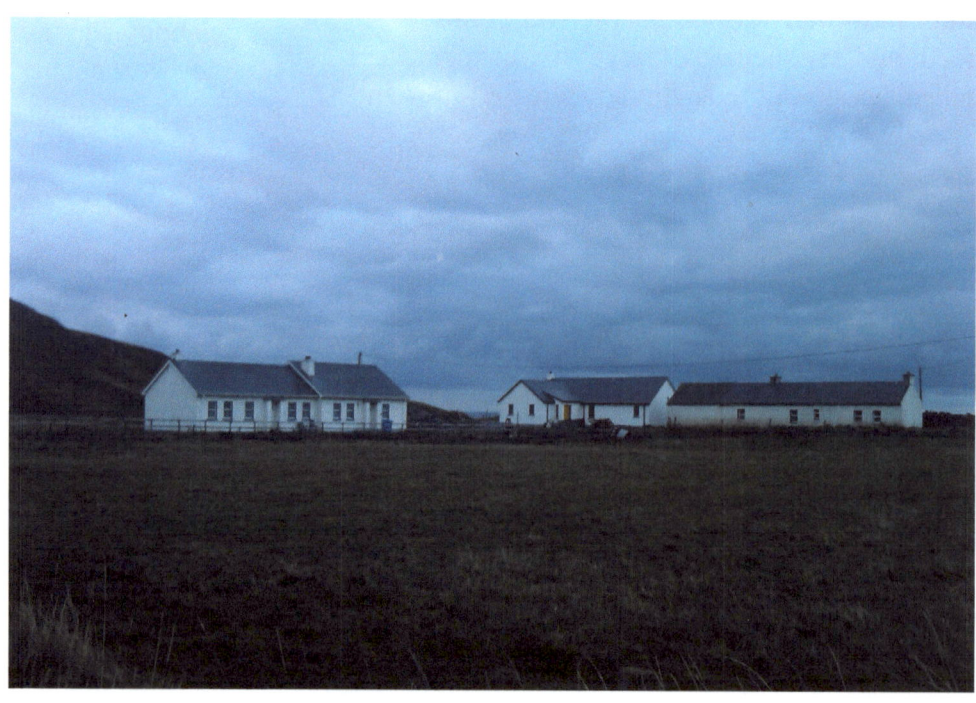

5 SUMMER, AUTUMN & FOLLOWING YEAR

The same year, 2003, at the end of October, I was a guest on the BBC radio station, BBC Radio Foyle, in Derry, Northern Ireland, talking about my book, *Donegal Fairy Stories*. I'd returned rather late at night, around eleven PM, and, as I walked past the door to the laundry room, I had another one fly by my head at great speed.

She was sitting inside the circle and they were in the tall grass. They settled into the grass while one flew quickly by her right side and was gone. The other four rose from the grass and then settled back down, then rose again. One of the four flew towards her, and hovered about a foot from her face, then went back to the ground and another one flew slowly past her left side. The rest of them flew away, more slowly than either of the two that had flown by her.

Be that as it may, I have not seen them since, nor has Karlene.

I do continue to watch for them, particularly at the "magical" times of the year, the Vernal and Autumnal Equinoxes.

I keep my camera ready.

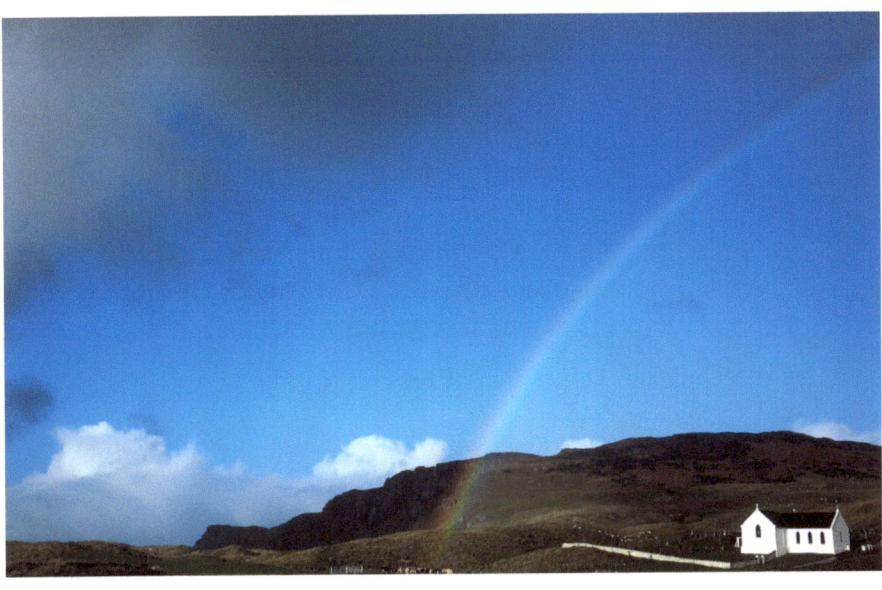

Left, rainbow over Lagg Church, near Trawbreaga Bay.

Below, the surf near our house, Malin Head.

One woman to whom I told the story was convinced that the fairies knew that I believed in them and had written the book of Donegal Fairy Stories and that they were showing their gratitude by appearing to me.

There is a small hill between the house and the road, on which we have stood up the largest stones we could move, and formed our own "fairy circle." The next year, in the Summer of 2004, my wife Karlene saw five fairies that she said looked like the ones in the photographs, at dusk, at the fairy circle's edge.

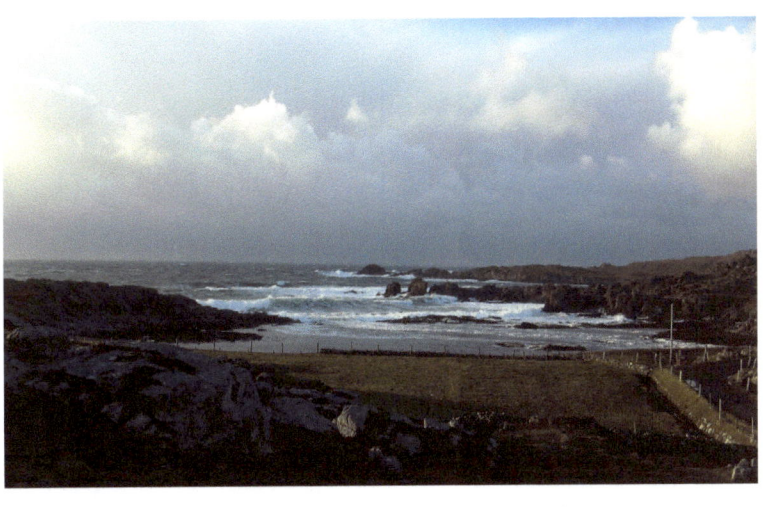

ABOUT THE AUTHOR

J.A. Greenleaf is a former sailor, Polar explorer, military officer, policeman and lawyer. He is a Michigan Master Lawyer. Joe has degrees in Political Science, minoring in English, a Juris Doctor in Law and a Masters of Law in Information Technology and Telecommunications Law from the University

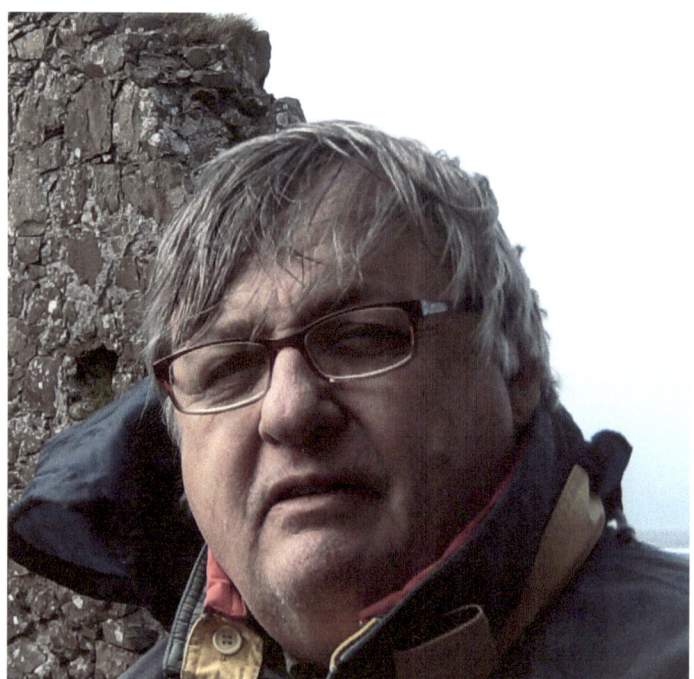

of Strathclyde in Glasgow, Scotland. He resides in Malin Head, Co Donegal, Ireland with his wife, Karlene. They also have a home in the Omaha, Nebraska, USA, area. He is a full-time author. He is the editor of *Donegal Fairy Stories,* by Seumas MacManus, and is the author of *Sudden Light: Donegal's Novel,* the first of series of four novels spanning four hundred years of Irish and world history. Currently, he is working on a sequel to *Sudden Light,* six novels, and a clinical book about Asperger's Syndrome, entitled, *Tell Them I'm Not Crazy,* to be published soon. His website is www.jagreenleaf.com and he can be reached by email at joe@jagreenleaf.com.

APPENDIX

The following pages display full page images of each of the five fairy photographs, in the order they were taken. The first one was taken at 23:27:51 hours (11:27:51 PM), the second at 23:28:27, the third at 23:28:37, the fourth at 23:29:03 and the fifth and final photograph was taken at 23:29:18. Less than two minutes transpired between the first and the last. None of the photographs were edited, Photoshopped or modified in any way.

Subsequent images are enlargements of sections of each photograph, showing the greatest enlargement without undue pixelation and distortion. The enlargements were accomplished using Photoshop CS6, and the only function was to enlarge and not edited or modify in any manner.

Following the photographs are digital camera information, Exchangeable Image File Format or EXIF. This information was created by the camera. All of the EXIF information is provided. Some is important; most is not.

The images, 1-5, are numbered 0000, 0001, 0002, 0003 and 0004.

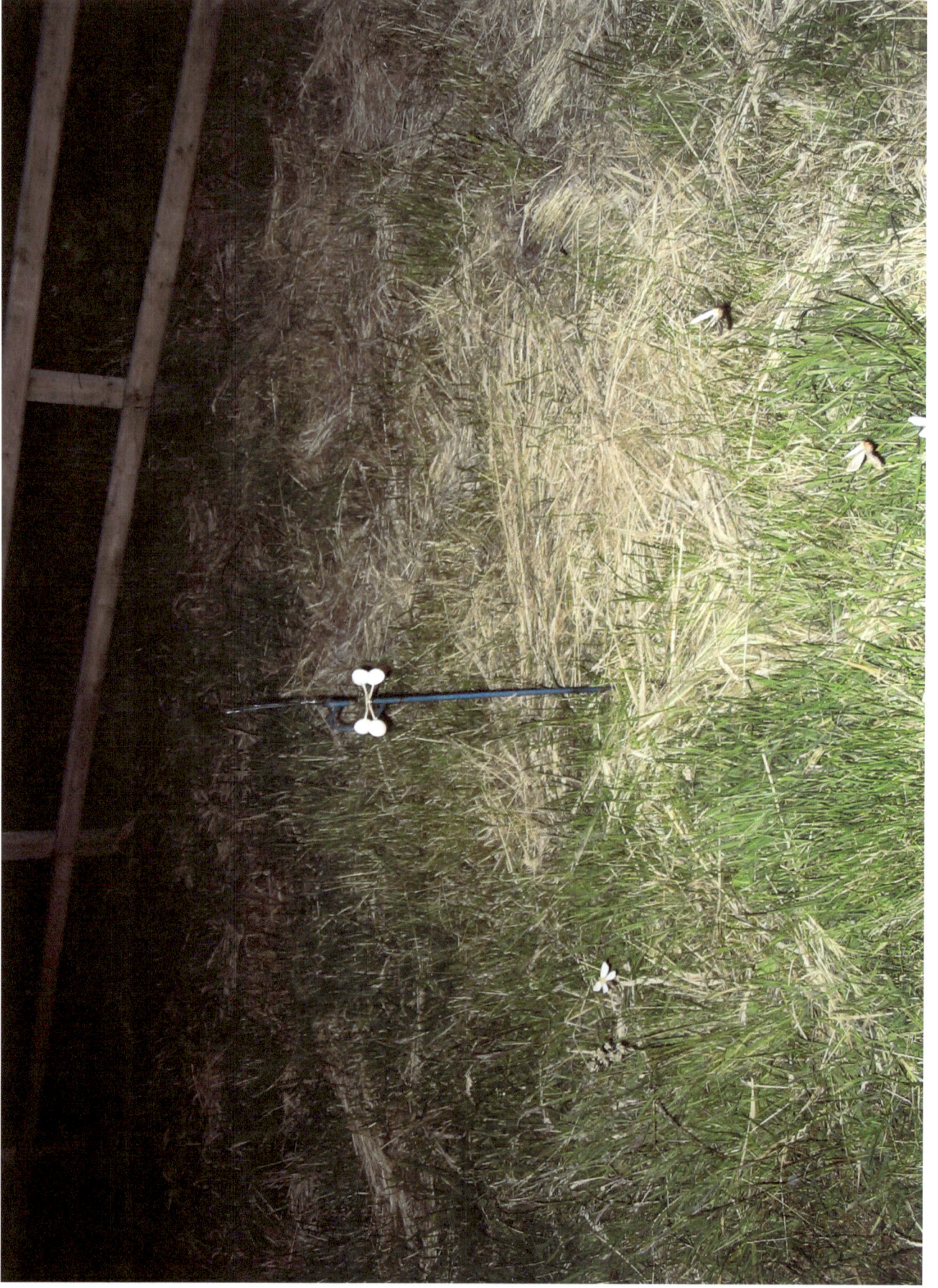

15

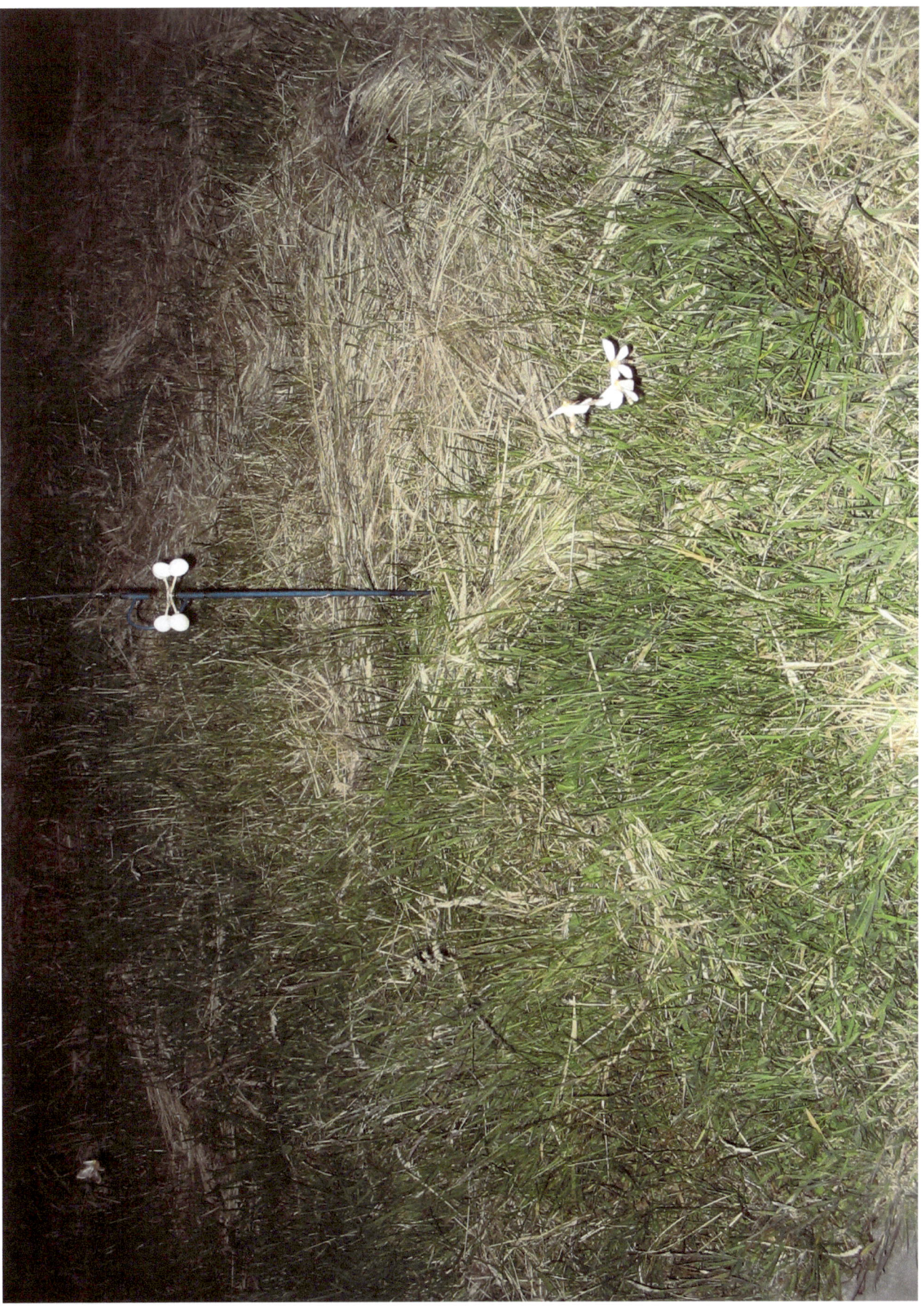

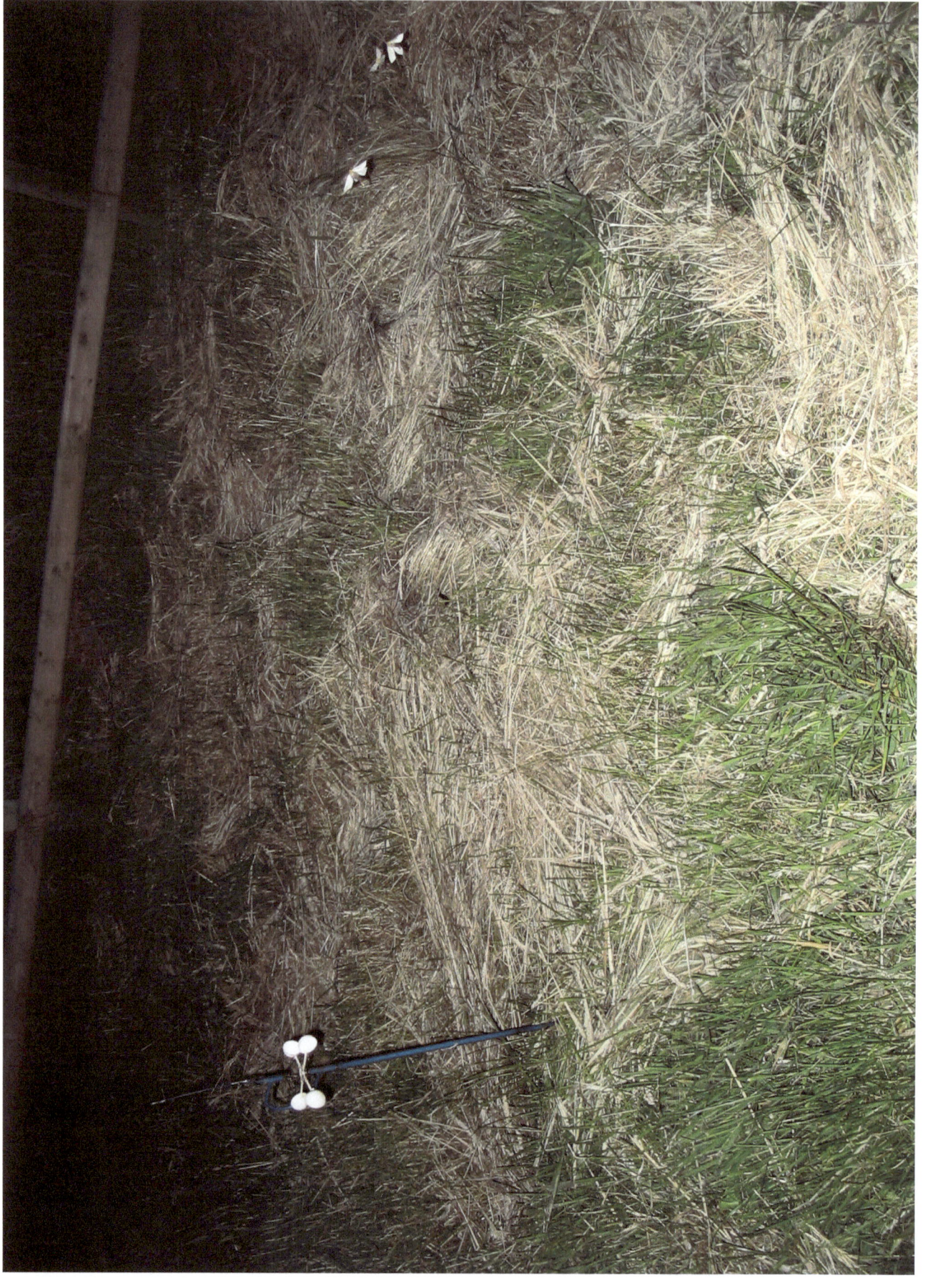

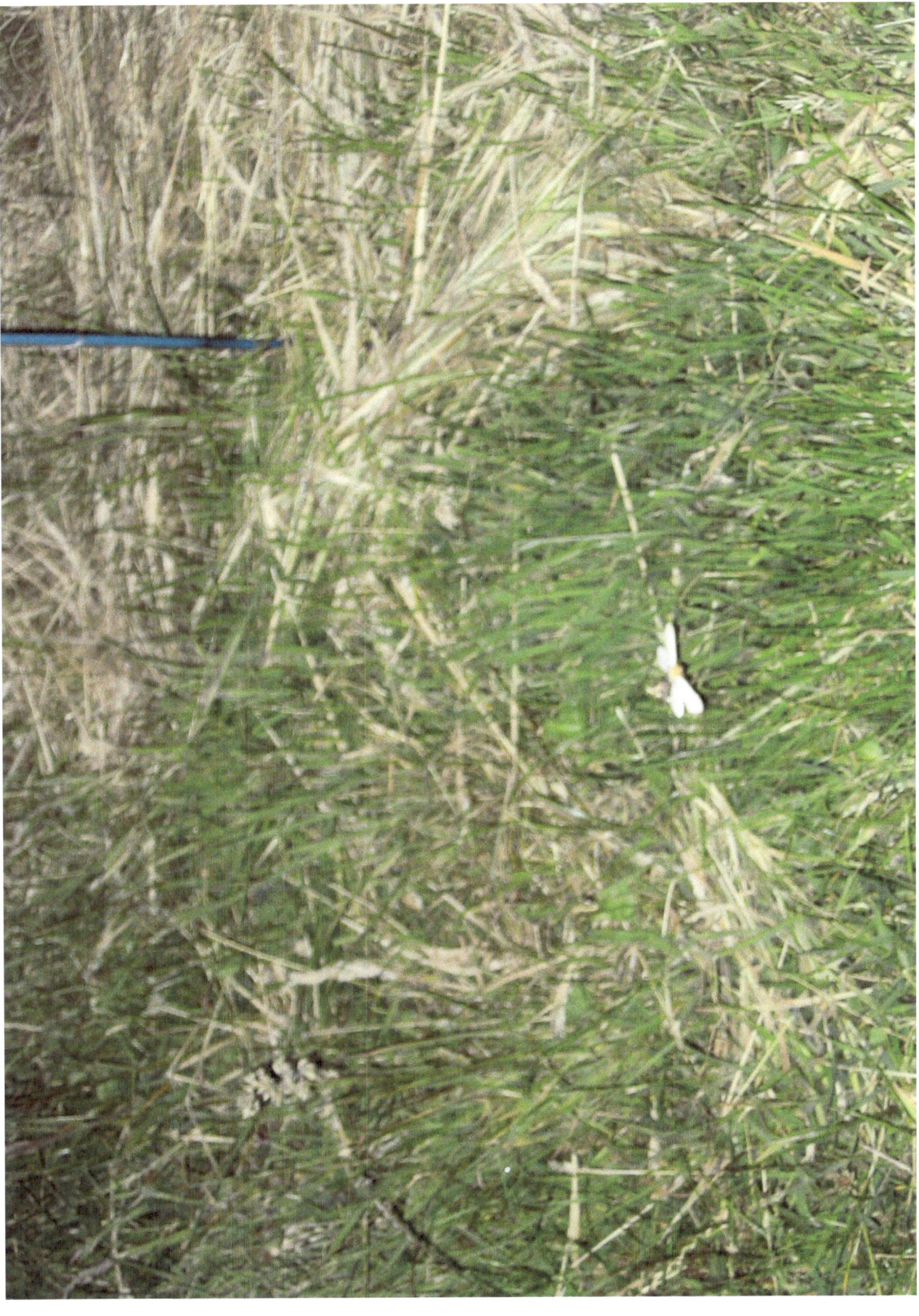

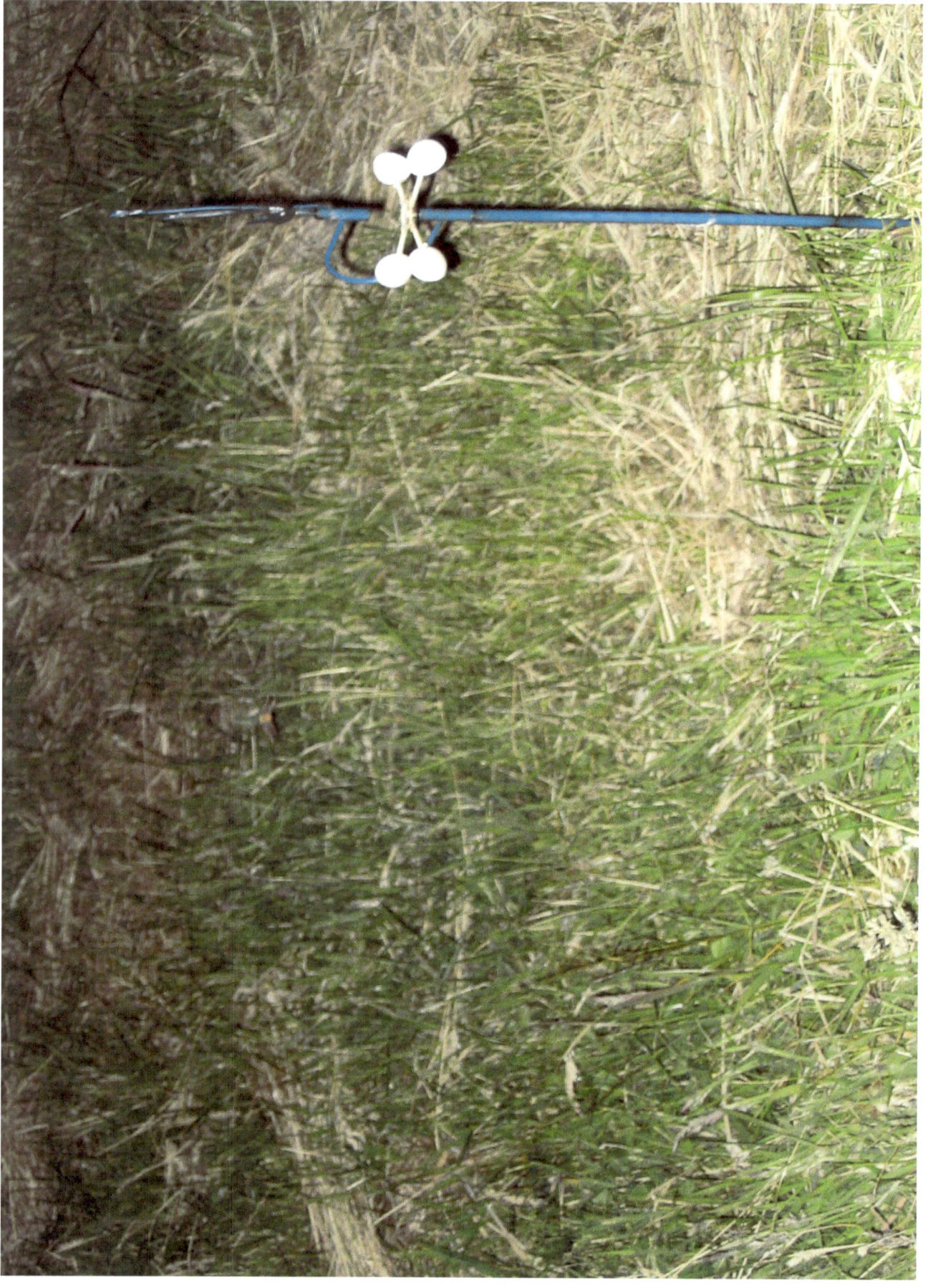

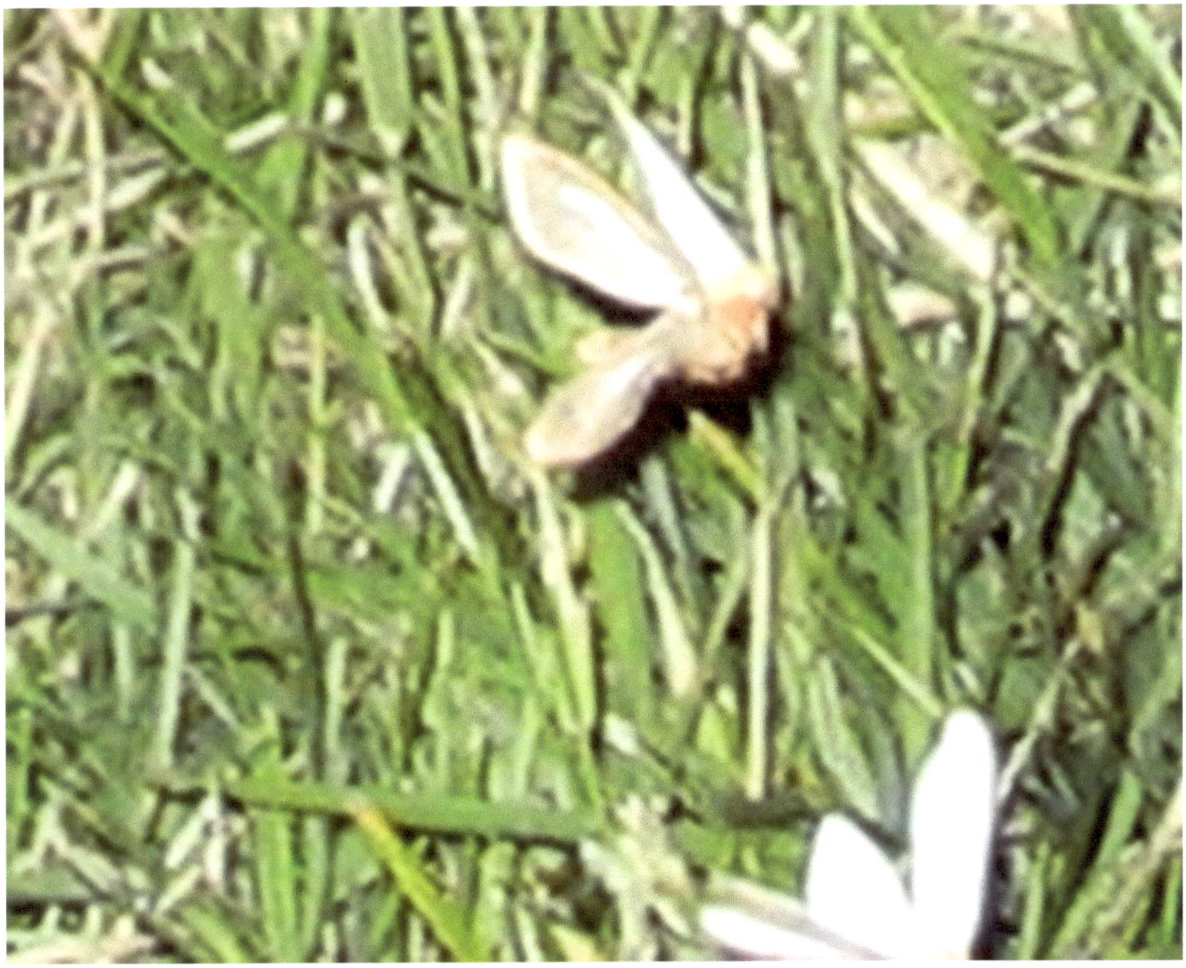

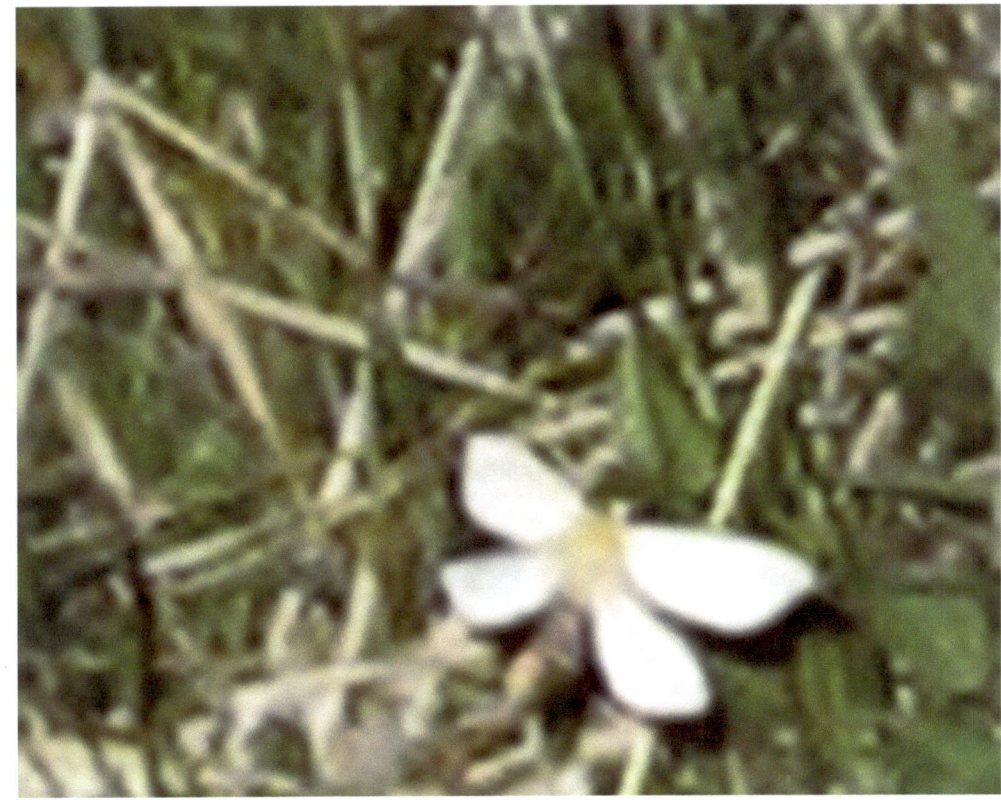

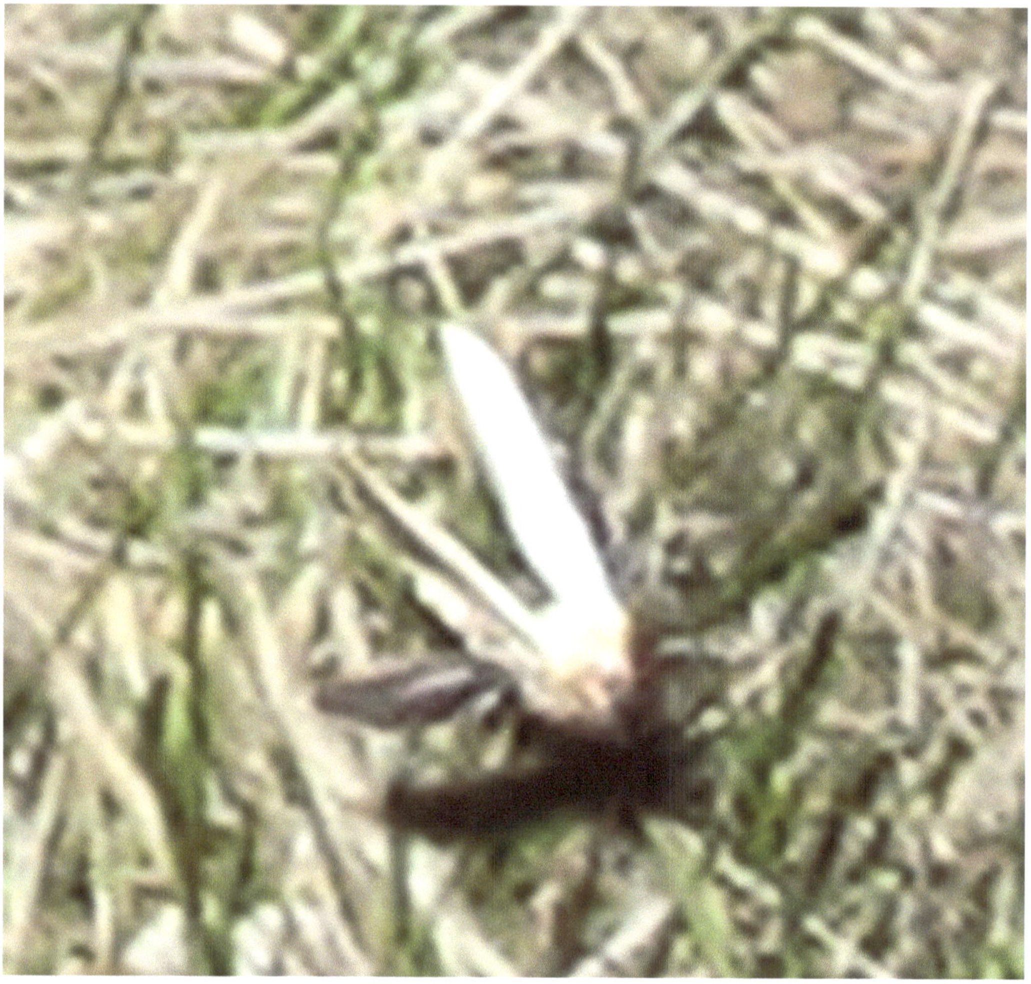

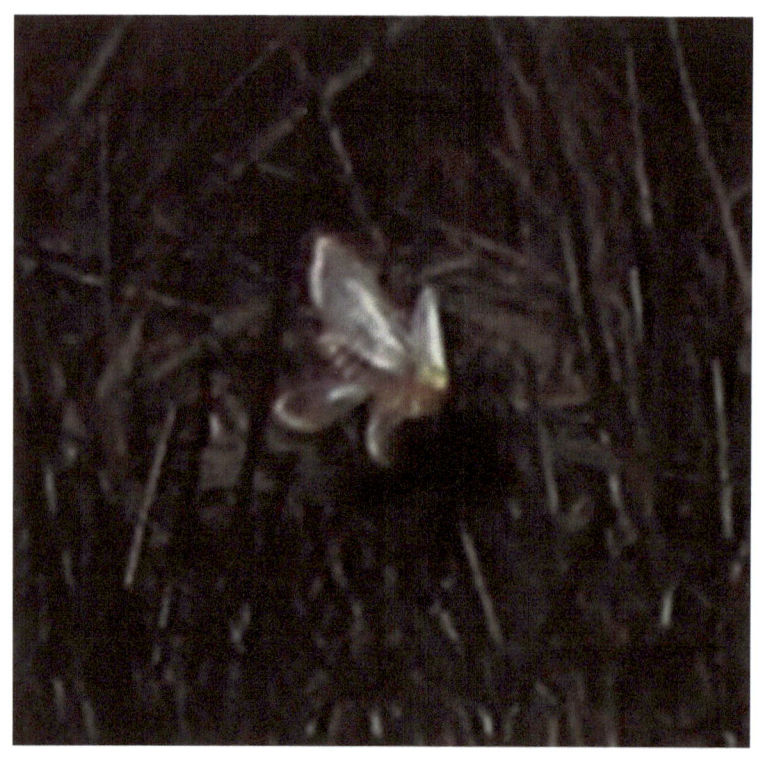

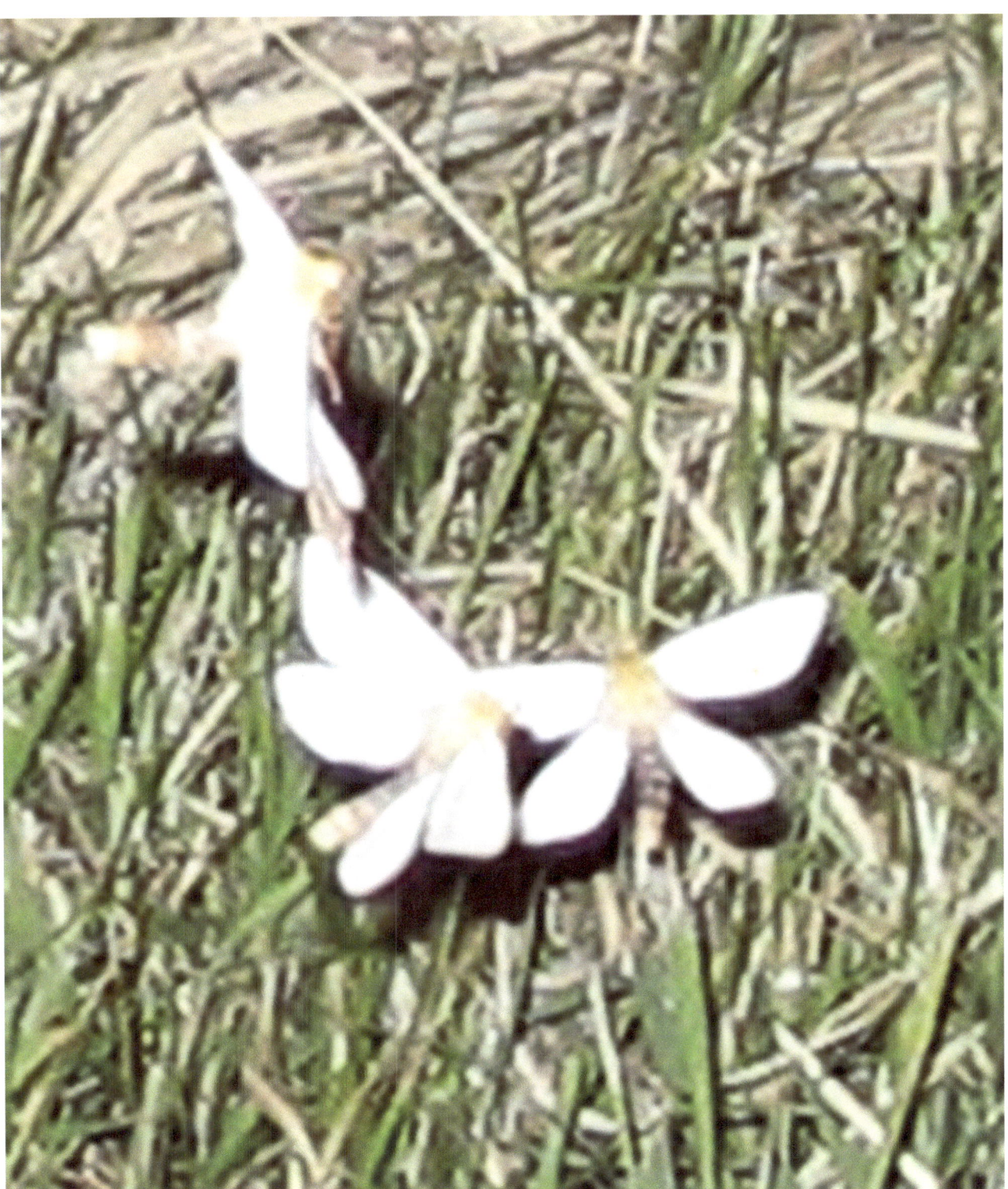

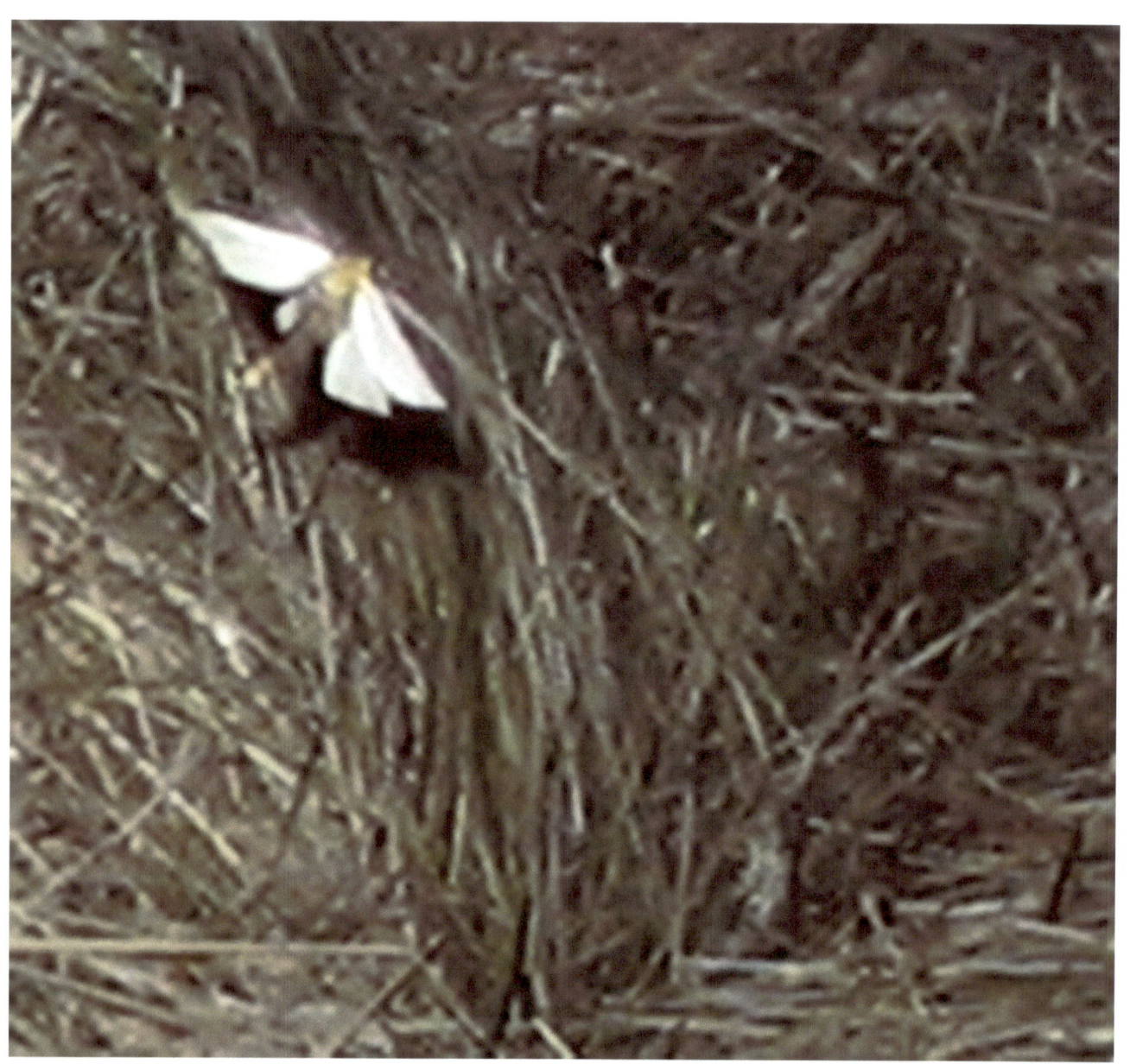

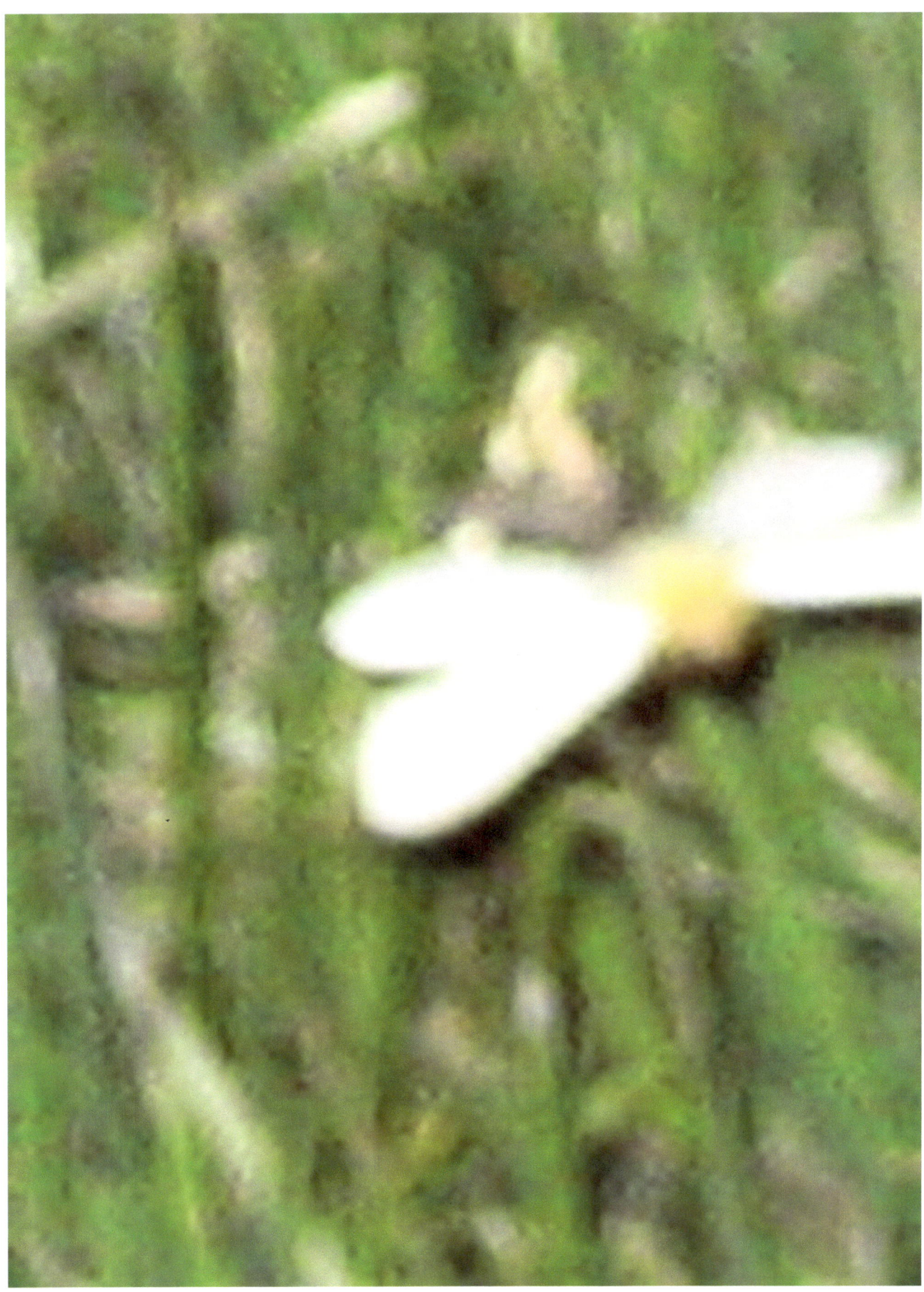

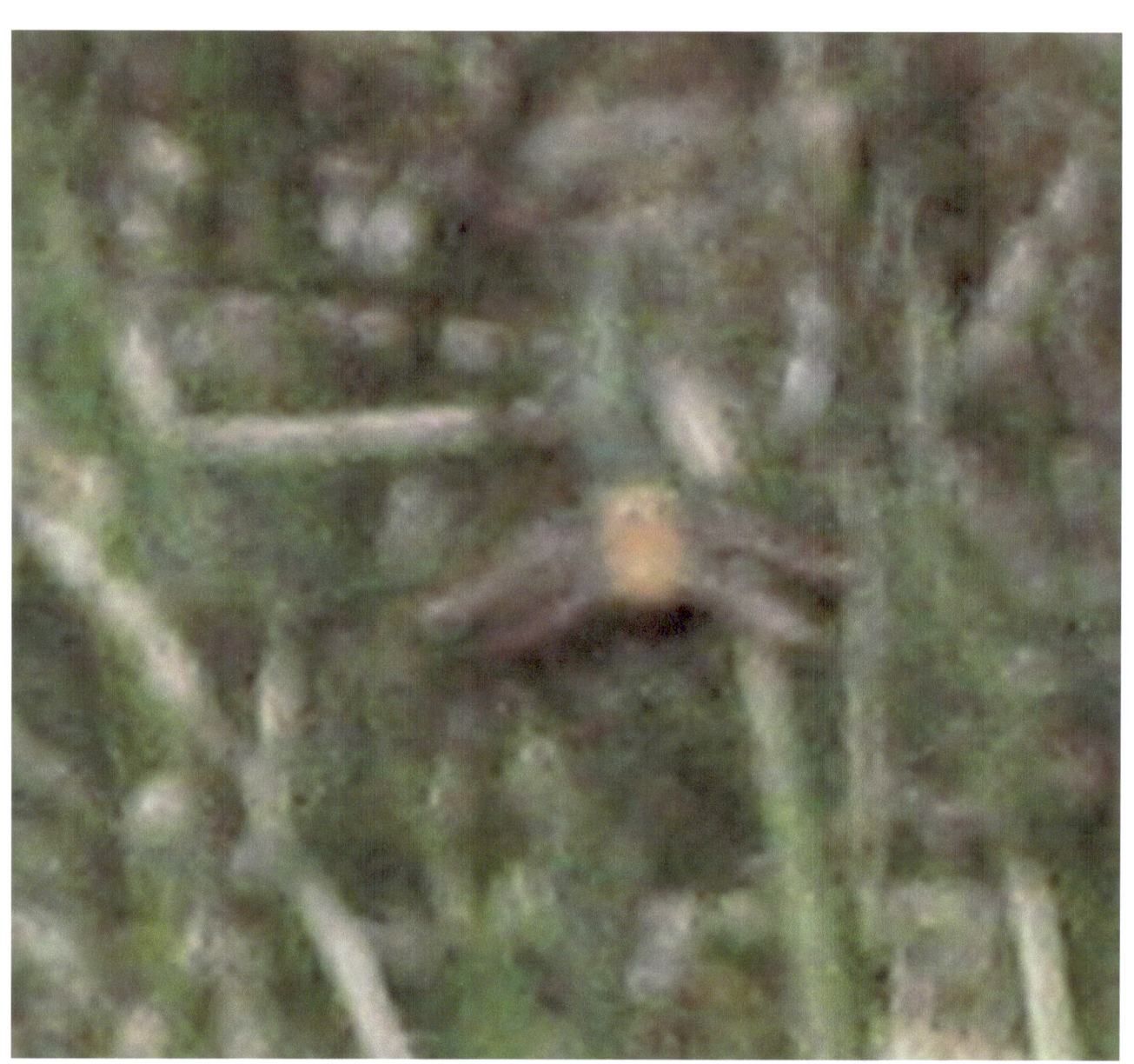

EXIF DATA

EXIF is "exchangeable image file format." Essentially, the different digital cameras record and save a wide variety of information about each photograph. If the camera has GPS (Global Positioning Satellite) capabilities (unlike the camera I used to take these photographs), EXIF will also include the geographical position (latitude and longitude) of the photograph. A great deal of the EXIF information is of interest and use only to experts.

Here follows EXIF for each of the five photographs, unedited.

Filename = Captured 2003-6-21 00000.JPG
Exif.Image.Make = Canon
Exif.Image.Model = Canon PowerShot A70
Exif.Image.Orientation = 1
Exif.Image.XResolution = 180/1
Exif.Image.YResolution = 180/1
Exif.Image.ResolutionUnit = 2
Exif.Image.DateTime = 2003:06:21 23:27:51
Exif.Image.YCbCrPositioning = 1
Exif.Image.ExifTag = 196
Exif.Photo.ExposureTime = 10/10
Exif.Photo.FNumber = 28/10
Exif.Photo.ExifVersion = 48 50 50 48
Exif.Photo.DateTimeOriginal = 2003:06:21 23:27:51
Exif.Photo.DateTimeDigitized = 2003:06:21 23:27:51
Exif.Photo.ComponentsConfiguration = 1 2 3 0
Exif.Photo.CompressedBitsPerPixel = 3/1
Exif.Photo.ShutterSpeedValue = 0/32
Exif.Photo.ApertureValue = 95/32
Exif.Photo.ExposureBiasValue = 0/3
Exif.Photo.MaxApertureValue = 95/32
Exif.Photo.MeteringMode =
Exif.Photo.Flash = 89
Exif.Photo.FocalLength = 173/32
Exif.Photo.UserComment = ################

##
##
##
##
##
################################
Exif.Photo.FlashpixVersion = 48 49 48 48
Exif.Photo.ColorSpace = 1
Exif.Photo.PixelXDimension = 2048
Exif.Photo.PixelYDimension = 1536
Exif.Photo.InteroperabilityTag = 1540
Exif.Photo.FocalPlaneXResolution = 2048000/208
Exif.Photo.FocalPlaneYResolution = 1536000/156
Exif.Photo.FocalPlaneResolutionUnit = 2
Exif.Photo.SensingMethod = 2
Exif.Photo.FileSource = 3
Exif.Photo.CustomRendered = 0
Exif.Photo.ExposureMode = 0
Exif.Photo.WhiteBalance = 0
Exif.Photo.DigitalZoomRatio = 2048/2048
Exif.Photo.SceneCaptureType = 3
Exif.Iop.InteroperabilityIndex = R98
Exif.Iop.InteroperabilityVersion = 48 49 48 48
Exif.Iop.RelatedImageWidth = 2048
Exif.Iop.RelatedImageLength = 1536
Exif.Thumbnail.Compression = 6
Exif.Thumbnail.XResolution = 180/1
Exif.Thumbnail.YResolution = 180/1
Exif.Thumbnail.ResolutionUnit = 2
Exif.Thumbnail.JPEGInterchangeFormat = 0
Exif.Thumbnail.JPEGInterchangeFormatLength = 4659
Exif.Canon.0x0002 = 2 173 213 159
Exif.Canon.0x0003 = 36 987 0 0
Exif.Canon.0x0000 = 0 0 0 0 0 0
Exif.Canon.0x0000 = 0 0 0 0 0 0
Exif.Canon.0x0013 = 0 0 0 0
Exif.Canon.ImageType = IMG:PowerShot A70 JPEG
Exif.Canon.FirmwareVersion = Firmware Version 1.00
Exif.Canon.ImageNumber = 1010112
Exif.Canon.OwnerName =
Exif.Canon.0x0010 = 19202048
Exif.Canon.0x000d = 68 9 309 309 309 309 309 309 309 309 309 69 0 0 0 0 0 10 65504 65488 0 25

316 43 80 1031 1226 0 0 0 0 111 0 113

Exif.CanonCs.Macro = 2
Exif.CanonCs.Selftimer = 0
Exif.CanonCs.Quality = 3
Exif.CanonCs.FlashMode = 5
Exif.CanonCs.DriveMode = 0
Exif.CanonCs.0x0006 = 0
Exif.CanonCs.FocusMode = 4
Exif.CanonCs.0x0008 = 0
Exif.CanonCs.0x0009 = 1
Exif.CanonCs.ImageSize = 0
Exif.CanonCs.EasyMode = 5
Exif.CanonCs.DigitalZoom = 0
Exif.CanonCs.Contrast = 0
Exif.CanonCs.Saturation = 0
Exif.CanonCs.Sharpness = 0
Exif.CanonCs.ISOSpeed = 15
Exif.CanonCs.MeteringMode = 3
Exif.CanonCs.FocusType = 1
Exif.CanonCs.AFPoint = 16385
Exif.CanonCs.ExposureProgram = 0
Exif.CanonCs.0x0015 = 65535
Exif.CanonCs.0x0016 = 65535
Exif.CanonCs.Lens = 519 173 32
Exif.CanonCs.0x001a = 98
Exif.CanonCs.0x001b = 192
Exif.CanonCs.FlashActivity = 1
Exif.CanonCs.FlashDetails = 8200
Exif.CanonCs.0x001e = 0
Exif.CanonCs.0x001f = 0
Exif.CanonCs.FocusContinuous = 0
Exif.CanonCs.AESetting = 0
Exif.CanonCs.ImageStabilization = 65535
Exif.CanonCs.DisplayAperture = 0
Exif.CanonCs.ZoomSourceWidth = 2048
Exif.CanonCs.ZoomTargetWidth = 2048
Exif.CanonCs.0x0026 = 0
Exif.CanonCs.0x0027 = 1
Exif.CanonCs.PhotoEffect = 0
Exif.CanonCs.0x0029 = 0
Exif.CanonCs.ColorTone = 32767
Exif.CanonCs.0x002b = 0
Exif.CanonCs.0x002c = 1
Exif.CanonCs.0x002d = 0
Exif.CanonPi.0x0001 = 5
Exif.CanonPi.ImageWidth = 2048

Exif.CanonPi.ImageHeight = 1536
Exif.CanonPi.ImageWidthAsShot = 2048
Exif.CanonPi.ImageHeightAsShot = 256
Exif.CanonPi.0x0006 = 369
Exif.CanonPi.0x0007 = 42
Exif.CanonPi.0x0008 = 0
Exif.CanonPi.0x0009 = 65166
Exif.CanonPi.0x000a = 0
Exif.CanonPi.0x000b = 370
Exif.CanonPi.0x000c = 0
Exif.CanonPi.0x000d = 65488
Exif.CanonPi.0x000e = 0
Exif.CanonPi.0x000f = 0
Exif.CanonPi.0x0010 = 0
Exif.CanonPi.0x0011 = 48
Exif.CanonPi.0x0012 = 0
Exif.CanonPi.0x0013 = 0
Exif.CanonSi.0x0001 = 0
Exif.CanonSi.ISOSpeed = 128
Exif.CanonSi.0x0003 = 65224
Exif.CanonSi.TargetAperture = 95
Exif.CanonSi.TargetShutterSpeed = 0
Exif.CanonSi.0x0006 = 0
Exif.CanonSi.WhiteBalance = 0
Exif.CanonSi.0x0008 = 1
Exif.CanonSi.Sequence = 0
Exif.CanonSi.0x000a = 0
Exif.CanonSi.0x000b = 0
Exif.CanonSi.0x000c = 0
Exif.CanonSi.0x000d = 288
Exif.CanonSi.AFPointUsed = 0
Exif.CanonSi.FlashBias = 0
Exif.CanonSi.0x0010 = 0
Exif.CanonSi.0x0011 = 0
Exif.CanonSi.0x0012 = 1
Exif.CanonSi.SubjectDistance = 84
Exif.CanonSi.0x0014 = 0
Exif.CanonSi.ApertureValue = 98
Exif.CanonSi.ShutterSpeedValue = 0
Exif.CanonSi.0x0017 = 0
Exif.CanonSi.0x0018 = 0
Exif.CanonSi.0x0019 = 65488
Exif.CanonSi.0x001a = 250
Exif.CanonSi.0x001b = 0
Exif.CanonSi.0x001c = 0

Exif.CanonSi.0x001d = 0
Exif.CanonSi.0x001e = 0
Exif.CanonSi.0x001f = 0
Exif.CanonSi.0x0020 = 0
Exif.CanonSi.0x0021 = 800

Filename = Captured 2003-6-21 00001.JPG
Exif.Image.Make = Canon
Exif.Image.Model = Canon PowerShot A70
Exif.Image.Orientation = 1
Exif.Image.XResolution = 180/1
Exif.Image.YResolution = 180/1
Exif.Image.ResolutionUnit = 2
Exif.Image.DateTime = 2003:06:21 23:28:27
Exif.Image.YCbCrPositioning = 1
Exif.Image.ExifTag = 196
Exif.Photo.ExposureTime = 10/10
Exif.Photo.FNumber = 28/10
Exif.Photo.ExifVersion = 48 50 50 48
Exif.Photo.DateTimeOriginal = 2003:06:21
23:28:27
Exif.Photo.DateTimeDigitized = 2003:06:21
23:28:27
Exif.Photo.ComponentsConfiguration = 1 2 3 0
Exif.Photo.CompressedBitsPerPixel = 3/1
Exif.Photo.ShutterSpeedValue = 0/32
Exif.Photo.ApertureValue = 95/32
Exif.Photo.ExposureBiasValue = 0/3
Exif.Photo.MaxApertureValue = 95/32
Exif.Photo.MeteringMode = 5
Exif.Photo.Flash = 89
Exif.Photo.FocalLength = 173/32
Exif.Photo.UserComment = ################
###
###
###
###
###
###############################
Exif.Photo.FlashpixVersion = 48 49 48 48
Exif.Photo.ColorSpace = 1
Exif.Photo.PixelXDimension = 2048
Exif.Photo.PixelYDimension = 1536
Exif.Photo.InteroperabilityTag = 1540
Exif.Photo.FocalPlaneXResolution =
2048000/208

Exif.Photo.FocalPlaneYResolution =
1536000/156
Exif.Photo.FocalPlaneResolutionUnit = 2
Exif.Photo.SensingMethod = 2
Exif.Photo.FileSource = 3
Exif.Photo.CustomRendered = 0
Exif.Photo.ExposureMode = 0
Exif.Photo.WhiteBalance = 0
Exif.Photo.DigitalZoomRatio = 2048/2048
Exif.Photo.SceneCaptureType = 3
Exif.Iop.InteroperabilityIndex = R98
Exif.Iop.InteroperabilityVersion = 48 49 48 48
Exif.Iop.RelatedImageWidth = 2048
Exif.Iop.RelatedImageLength = 1536
Exif.Thumbnail.Compression = 6
Exif.Thumbnail.XResolution = 180/1
Exif.Thumbnail.YResolution = 180/1
Exif.Thumbnail.ResolutionUnit = 2
Exif.Thumbnail.JPEGInterchangeFormat = 0
Exif.Thumbnail.JPEGInterchangeFormatLength
= 4790
Exif.Canon.0x0002 = 2 173 213 159
Exif.Canon.0x0003 = 35 988 0 0
Exif.Canon.0x0000 = 0 0 0 0 0 0
Exif.Canon.0x0000 = 0 0 0 0 0 0
Exif.Canon.0x0013 = 0 0 0 0
Exif.Canon.ImageType = IMG:PowerShot A70
JPEG
Exif.Canon.FirmwareVersion = Firmware Version 1.00
Exif.Canon.ImageNumber = 1010113
Exif.Canon.OwnerName =
Exif.Canon.0x0010 = 19202048
Exif.Canon.0x000d = 68 9 306 306 306 306 306
306 306 306 306 69 0 0 0 0 0 10 65504 65488 0
882 396 41 80 1033 1184 0 0 0 0 122 0 101
Exif.CanonCs.Macro = 2
Exif.CanonCs.Selftimer = 0
Exif.CanonCs.Quality = 3
Exif.CanonCs.FlashMode = 5
Exif.CanonCs.DriveMode = 0
Exif.CanonCs.0x0006 = 0
Exif.CanonCs.FocusMode = 4
Exif.CanonCs.0x0008 = 0
Exif.CanonCs.0x0009 = 1
Exif.CanonCs.ImageSize = 0

Exif.CanonCs.EasyMode = 5
Exif.CanonCs.DigitalZoom = 0
Exif.CanonCs.Contrast = 0
Exif.CanonCs.Saturation = 0
Exif.CanonCs.Sharpness = 0
Exif.CanonCs.ISOSpeed = 15
Exif.CanonCs.MeteringMode = 3
Exif.CanonCs.FocusType = 1
Exif.CanonCs.AFPoint = 16385
Exif.CanonCs.ExposureProgram = 0
Exif.CanonCs.0x0015 = 65535
Exif.CanonCs.0x0016 = 65535
Exif.CanonCs.Lens = 519 173 32
Exif.CanonCs.0x001a = 98
Exif.CanonCs.0x001b = 192
Exif.CanonCs.FlashActivity = 1
Exif.CanonCs.FlashDetails = 8200
Exif.CanonCs.0x001e = 0
Exif.CanonCs.0x001f = 0
Exif.CanonCs.FocusContinuous = 0
Exif.CanonCs.AESetting = 0
Exif.CanonCs.ImageStabilization = 65535
Exif.CanonCs.DisplayAperture = 0
Exif.CanonCs.ZoomSourceWidth = 2048
Exif.CanonCs.ZoomTargetWidth = 2048
Exif.CanonCs.0x0026 = 0
Exif.CanonCs.0x0027 = 1
Exif.CanonCs.PhotoEffect = 0
Exif.CanonCs.0x0029 = 0
Exif.CanonCs.ColorTone = 32767
Exif.CanonCs.0x002b = 0
Exif.CanonCs.0x002c = 1
Exif.CanonCs.0x002d = 0
Exif.CanonPi.0x0001 = 5
Exif.CanonPi.ImageWidth = 2048
Exif.CanonPi.ImageHeight = 1536
Exif.CanonPi.ImageWidthAsShot = 2048
Exif.CanonPi.ImageHeightAsShot = 256
Exif.CanonPi.0x0006 = 369
Exif.CanonPi.0x0007 = 42
Exif.CanonPi.0x0008 = 0
Exif.CanonPi.0x0009 = 65166
Exif.CanonPi.0x000a = 0
Exif.CanonPi.0x000b = 370
Exif.CanonPi.0x000c = 0
Exif.CanonPi.0x000d = 65488

Exif.CanonPi.0x000e = 0
Exif.CanonPi.0x000f = 0
Exif.CanonPi.0x0010 = 0
Exif.CanonPi.0x0011 = 48
Exif.CanonPi.0x0012 = 0
Exif.CanonPi.0x0013 = 0
Exif.CanonSi.0x0001 = 0
Exif.CanonSi.ISOSpeed = 128
Exif.CanonSi.0x0003 = 65224
Exif.CanonSi.TargetAperture = 95
Exif.CanonSi.TargetShutterSpeed = 0
Exif.CanonSi.0x0006 = 0
Exif.CanonSi.WhiteBalance = 0
Exif.CanonSi.0x0008 = 1
Exif.CanonSi.Sequence = 0
Exif.CanonSi.0x000a = 0
Exif.CanonSi.0x000b = 0
Exif.CanonSi.0x000c = 0
Exif.CanonSi.0x000d = 272
Exif.CanonSi.AFPointUsed = 0
Exif.CanonSi.FlashBias = 0
Exif.CanonSi.0x0010 = 0
Exif.CanonSi.0x0011 = 0
Exif.CanonSi.0x0012 = 1
Exif.CanonSi.SubjectDistance = 139
Exif.CanonSi.0x0014 = 0
Exif.CanonSi.ApertureValue = 98
Exif.CanonSi.ShutterSpeedValue = 0
Exif.CanonSi.0x0017 = 0
Exif.CanonSi.0x0018 = 0
Exif.CanonSi.0x0019 = 65488
Exif.CanonSi.0x001a = 250
Exif.CanonSi.0x001b = 0
Exif.CanonSi.0x001c = 0
Exif.CanonSi.0x001d = 0
Exif.CanonSi.0x001e = 0
Exif.CanonSi.0x001f = 0
Exif.CanonSi.0x0020 = 0
Exif.CanonSi.0x0021 = 250

Filename = Captured 2003-6-21 00002.JPG
Exif.Image.Make = Canon
Exif.Image.Model = Canon PowerShot A70
Exif.Image.Orientation = 1
Exif.Image.XResolution = 180/1
Exif.Image.YResolution = 180/1

Exif.Image.ResolutionUnit = 2
Exif.Image.DateTime = 2003:06:21 23:28:37
Exif.Image.YCbCrPositioning = 1
Exif.Image.ExifTag = 196
Exif.Photo.ExposureTime = 10/10
Exif.Photo.FNumber = 28/10
Exif.Photo.ExifVersion = 48 50 50 48
Exif.Photo.DateTimeOriginal = 2003:06:21 23:28:37
Exif.Photo.DateTimeDigitized = 2003:06:21 23:28:37
Exif.Photo.ComponentsConfiguration = 1 2 3 0
Exif.Photo.CompressedBitsPerPixel = 3/1
Exif.Photo.ShutterSpeedValue = 0/32
Exif.Photo.ApertureValue = 95/32
Exif.Photo.ExposureBiasValue = 0/3
Exif.Photo.MaxApertureValue = 95/32
Exif.Photo.MeteringMode = 5
Exif.Photo.Flash = 89
Exif.Photo.FocalLength = 173/32
Exif.Photo.UserComment = ##################
##
##
##
##
##
################################
Exif.Photo.FlashpixVersion = 48 49 48 48
Exif.Photo.ColorSpace = 1
Exif.Photo.PixelXDimension = 2048
Exif.Photo.PixelYDimension = 1536
Exif.Photo.InteroperabilityTag = 1540
Exif.Photo.FocalPlaneXResolution = 2048000/208
Exif.Photo.FocalPlaneYResolution = 1536000/156
Exif.Photo.FocalPlaneResolutionUnit = 2
Exif.Photo.SensingMethod = 2
Exif.Photo.FileSource = 3
Exif.Photo.CustomRendered = 0
Exif.Photo.ExposureMode = 0
Exif.Photo.WhiteBalance = 0
Exif.Photo.DigitalZoomRatio = 2048/2048
Exif.Photo.SceneCaptureType = 3
Exif.Iop.InteroperabilityIndex = R98
Exif.Iop.InteroperabilityVersion = 48 49 48 48
Exif.Iop.RelatedImageWidth = 2048
Exif.Iop.RelatedImageLength = 1536

Exif.Thumbnail.Compression = 6
Exif.Thumbnail.XResolution = 180/1
Exif.Thumbnail.YResolution = 180/1
Exif.Thumbnail.ResolutionUnit = 2
Exif.Thumbnail.JPEGInterchangeFormat = 0
Exif.Thumbnail.JPEGInterchangeFormatLength = 4630
Exif.Canon.0x0002 = 2 173 213 159
Exif.Canon.0x0003 = 31 992 0 0
Exif.Canon.0x0000 = 0 0 0 0 0 0
Exif.Canon.0x0000 = 0 0 0 0 0 0
Exif.Canon.0x0013 = 0 0 0 0
Exif.Canon.ImageType = IMG:PowerShot A70 JPEG
Exif.Canon.FirmwareVersion = Firmware Version 1.00
Exif.Canon.ImageNumber = 1010114
Exif.Canon.OwnerName =
Exif.Canon.0x0010 = 19202048
Exif.Canon.0x000d = 68 9 306 306 306 306 306 306 306 306 306 69 0 0 0 0 0 10 65504 65488 0 882 396 53 80 1034 1031 0 0 0 0 146 0 108
Exif.CanonCs.Macro = 2
Exif.CanonCs.Selftimer = 0
Exif.CanonCs.Quality = 3
Exif.CanonCs.FlashMode = 5
Exif.CanonCs.DriveMode = 0
Exif.CanonCs.0x0006 = 0
Exif.CanonCs.FocusMode = 4
Exif.CanonCs.0x0008 = 0
Exif.CanonCs.0x0009 = 1
Exif.CanonCs.ImageSize = 0
Exif.CanonCs.EasyMode = 5
Exif.CanonCs.DigitalZoom = 0
Exif.CanonCs.Contrast = 0
Exif.CanonCs.Saturation = 0
Exif.CanonCs.Sharpness = 0
Exif.CanonCs.ISOSpeed = 15
Exif.CanonCs.MeteringMode = 3
Exif.CanonCs.FocusType = 1
Exif.CanonCs.AFPoint = 16385
Exif.CanonCs.ExposureProgram = 0
Exif.CanonCs.0x0015 = 65535
Exif.CanonCs.0x0016 = 65535
Exif.CanonCs.Lens = 519 173 32
Exif.CanonCs.0x001a = 98

Exif.CanonCs.0x001b = 192
Exif.CanonCs.FlashActivity = 1
Exif.CanonCs.FlashDetails = 8200
Exif.CanonCs.0x001e = 0
Exif.CanonCs.0x001f = 0
Exif.CanonCs.FocusContinuous = 0
Exif.CanonCs.AESetting = 0
Exif.CanonCs.ImageStabilization = 65535
Exif.CanonCs.DisplayAperture = 0
Exif.CanonCs.ZoomSourceWidth = 2048
Exif.CanonCs.ZoomTargetWidth = 2048
Exif.CanonCs.0x0026 = 0
Exif.CanonCs.0x0027 = 1
Exif.CanonCs.PhotoEffect = 0
Exif.CanonCs.0x0029 = 0
Exif.CanonCs.ColorTone = 32767
Exif.CanonCs.0x002b = 0
Exif.CanonCs.0x002c = 1
Exif.CanonCs.0x002d = 0
Exif.CanonPi.0x0001 = 5
Exif.CanonPi.ImageWidth = 2048
Exif.CanonPi.ImageHeight = 1536
Exif.CanonPi.ImageWidthAsShot = 2048
Exif.CanonPi.ImageHeightAsShot = 256
Exif.CanonPi.0x0006 = 369
Exif.CanonPi.0x0007 = 42
Exif.CanonPi.0x0008 = 0
Exif.CanonPi.0x0009 = 65166
Exif.CanonPi.0x000a = 0
Exif.CanonPi.0x000b = 370
Exif.CanonPi.0x000c = 0
Exif.CanonPi.0x000d = 65488
Exif.CanonPi.0x000e = 0
Exif.CanonPi.0x000f = 0
Exif.CanonPi.0x0010 = 0
Exif.CanonPi.0x0011 = 48
Exif.CanonPi.0x0012 = 0
Exif.CanonPi.0x0013 = 0
Exif.CanonSi.0x0001 = 0
Exif.CanonSi.ISOSpeed = 128
Exif.CanonSi.0x0003 = 65224
Exif.CanonSi.TargetAperture = 95
Exif.CanonSi.TargetShutterSpeed = 0
Exif.CanonSi.0x0006 = 0
Exif.CanonSi.WhiteBalance = 0
Exif.CanonSi.0x0008 = 1

Exif.CanonSi.Sequence = 0
Exif.CanonSi.0x000a = 0
Exif.CanonSi.0x000b = 0
Exif.CanonSi.0x000c = 0
Exif.CanonSi.0x000d = 279
Exif.CanonSi.AFPointUsed = 0
Exif.CanonSi.FlashBias = 0
Exif.CanonSi.0x0010 = 0
Exif.CanonSi.0x0011 = 0
Exif.CanonSi.0x0012 = 1
Exif.CanonSi.SubjectDistance = 139
Exif.CanonSi.0x0014 = 0
Exif.CanonSi.ApertureValue = 98
Exif.CanonSi.ShutterSpeedValue = 0
Exif.CanonSi.0x0017 = 0
Exif.CanonSi.0x0018 = 0
Exif.CanonSi.0x0019 = 65488
Exif.CanonSi.0x001a = 250
Exif.CanonSi.0x001b = 0
Exif.CanonSi.0x001c = 0
Exif.CanonSi.0x001d = 0
Exif.CanonSi.0x001e = 0
Exif.CanonSi.0x001f = 0
Exif.CanonSi.0x0020 = 0
Exif.CanonSi.0x0021 = 366

Filename = Captured 2003-6-21 00003.JPG
Exif.Image.Make = Canon
Exif.Image.Model = Canon PowerShot A70
Exif.Image.Orientation = 1
Exif.Image.XResolution = 180/1
Exif.Image.YResolution = 180/1
Exif.Image.ResolutionUnit = 2
Exif.Image.DateTime = 2003:06:21 23:29:06
Exif.Image.YCbCrPositioning = 1
Exif.Image.ExifTag = 196
Exif.Photo.ExposureTime = 1/60
Exif.Photo.FNumber = 40/10
Exif.Photo.ExifVersion = 48 50 50 48
Exif.Photo.DateTimeOriginal = 2003:06:21
23:29:06
Exif.Photo.DateTimeDigitized = 2003:06:21
23:29:06
Exif.Photo.ComponentsConfiguration = 1 2 3 0
Exif.Photo.CompressedBitsPerPixel = 3/1
Exif.Photo.ShutterSpeedValue = 189/32

Exif.Photo.ApertureValue = 128/32
Exif.Photo.ExposureBiasValue = 0/3
Exif.Photo.MaxApertureValue = 128/32
Exif.Photo.MeteringMode = 5
Exif.Photo.Flash = 89
Exif.Photo.FocalLength = 362/32
Exif.Photo.UserComment = #################
##
##
##
##
##
#################################
Exif.Photo.FlashpixVersion = 48 49 48 48
Exif.Photo.ColorSpace = 1
Exif.Photo.PixelXDimension = 2048
Exif.Photo.PixelYDimension = 1536
Exif.Photo.InteroperabilityTag = 1540
Exif.Photo.FocalPlaneXResolution = 2048000/208
Exif.Photo.FocalPlaneYResolution = 1536000/156
Exif.Photo.FocalPlaneResolutionUnit = 2
Exif.Photo.SensingMethod = 2
Exif.Photo.FileSource = 3
Exif.Photo.CustomRendered = 0
Exif.Photo.ExposureMode = 0
Exif.Photo.WhiteBalance = 0
Exif.Photo.DigitalZoomRatio = 2048/2048
Exif.Photo.SceneCaptureType = 0
Exif.Iop.InteroperabilityIndex = R98
Exif.Iop.InteroperabilityVersion = 48 49 48 48
Exif.Iop.RelatedImageWidth = 2048
Exif.Iop.RelatedImageLength = 1536
Exif.Thumbnail.Compression = 6
Exif.Thumbnail.XResolution = 180/1
Exif.Thumbnail.YResolution = 180/1
Exif.Thumbnail.ResolutionUnit = 2
Exif.Thumbnail.JPEGInterchangeFormat = 0
Exif.Thumbnail.JPEGInterchangeFormatLength = 5793
Exif.Canon.0x0002 = 2 362 213 159
Exif.Canon.0x0003 = 0 1024 0 0
Exif.Canon.0x0000 = 0 0 0 0 0 0
Exif.Canon.0x0000 = 0 0 0 0 0 0
Exif.Canon.0x0013 = 0 0 0 0
Exif.Canon.ImageType = IMG:PowerShot A70 JPEG
Exif.Canon.FirmwareVersion = Firmware Version 1.00
Exif.Canon.ImageNumber = 1010115
Exif.Canon.OwnerName =
Exif.Canon.0x0010 = 19202048
Exif.Canon.0x000d = 68 9 271 271 271 271 271 271 271 271 271 69 0 0 0 0 10 65504 65488 0 882 396 32 80 1038 1194 0 0 0 0 113 0 76
Exif.CanonCs.Macro = 2
Exif.CanonCs.Selftimer = 0
Exif.CanonCs.Quality = 3
Exif.CanonCs.FlashMode = 5
Exif.CanonCs.DriveMode = 0
Exif.CanonCs.0x0006 = 0
Exif.CanonCs.FocusMode = 4
Exif.CanonCs.0x0008 = 0
Exif.CanonCs.0x0009 = 1
Exif.CanonCs.ImageSize = 0
Exif.CanonCs.EasyMode = 0
Exif.CanonCs.DigitalZoom = 0
Exif.CanonCs.Contrast = 0
Exif.CanonCs.Saturation = 0
Exif.CanonCs.Sharpness = 0
Exif.CanonCs.ISOSpeed = 15
Exif.CanonCs.MeteringMode = 3
Exif.CanonCs.FocusType = 1
Exif.CanonCs.AFPoint = 16385
Exif.CanonCs.ExposureProgram = 0
Exif.CanonCs.0x0015 = 65535
Exif.CanonCs.0x0016 = 65535
Exif.CanonCs.Lens = 519 173 32
Exif.CanonCs.0x001a = 129
Exif.CanonCs.0x001b = 192
Exif.CanonCs.FlashActivity = 1
Exif.CanonCs.FlashDetails = 8200
Exif.CanonCs.0x001e = 0
Exif.CanonCs.0x001f = 0
Exif.CanonCs.FocusContinuous = 0
Exif.CanonCs.AESetting = 0
Exif.CanonCs.ImageStabilization = 65535
Exif.CanonCs.DisplayAperture = 0
Exif.CanonCs.ZoomSourceWidth = 2048
Exif.CanonCs.ZoomTargetWidth = 2048
Exif.CanonCs.0x0026 = 0
Exif.CanonCs.0x0027 = 1
Exif.CanonCs.PhotoEffect = 0

Exif.CanonCs.0x0029 = 0
Exif.CanonCs.ColorTone = 32767
Exif.CanonCs.0x002b = 0
Exif.CanonCs.0x002c = 0
Exif.CanonCs.0x002d = 0
Exif.CanonPi.0x0001 = 5
Exif.CanonPi.ImageWidth = 2048
Exif.CanonPi.ImageHeight = 1536
Exif.CanonPi.ImageWidthAsShot = 2048
Exif.CanonPi.ImageHeightAsShot = 256
Exif.CanonPi.0x0006 = 369
Exif.CanonPi.0x0007 = 42
Exif.CanonPi.0x0008 = 0
Exif.CanonPi.0x0009 = 65166
Exif.CanonPi.0x000a = 0
Exif.CanonPi.0x000b = 370
Exif.CanonPi.0x000c = 0
Exif.CanonPi.0x000d = 65488
Exif.CanonPi.0x000e = 0
Exif.CanonPi.0x000f = 0
Exif.CanonPi.0x0010 = 0
Exif.CanonPi.0x0011 = 48
Exif.CanonPi.0x0012 = 0
Exif.CanonPi.0x0013 = 0
Exif.CanonSi.0x0001 = 48
Exif.CanonSi.ISOSpeed = 128
Exif.CanonSi.0x0003 = 65255
Exif.CanonSi.TargetAperture = 128
Exif.CanonSi.TargetShutterSpeed = 189
Exif.CanonSi.0x0006 = 0
Exif.CanonSi.WhiteBalance = 0
Exif.CanonSi.0x0008 = 0
Exif.CanonSi.Sequence = 0
Exif.CanonSi.0x000a = 4
Exif.CanonSi.0x000b = 0
Exif.CanonSi.0x000c = 0
Exif.CanonSi.0x000d = 236
Exif.CanonSi.AFPointUsed = 0
Exif.CanonSi.FlashBias = 0
Exif.CanonSi.0x0010 = 0
Exif.CanonSi.0x0011 = 0
Exif.CanonSi.0x0012 = 1
Exif.CanonSi.SubjectDistance = 101
Exif.CanonSi.0x0014 = 0
Exif.CanonSi.ApertureValue = 129
Exif.CanonSi.ShutterSpeedValue = 192

Exif.CanonSi.0x0017 = 0
Exif.CanonSi.0x0018 = 0
Exif.CanonSi.0x0019 = 65488
Exif.CanonSi.0x001a = 250
Exif.CanonSi.0x001b = 0
Exif.CanonSi.0x001c = 0
Exif.CanonSi.0x001d = 0
Exif.CanonSi.0x001e = 0
Exif.CanonSi.0x001f = 0
Exif.CanonSi.0x0020 = 0
Exif.CanonSi.0x0021 = 111

Filename = Captured 2003-6-21 00004.JPG
Exif.Image.Make = Canon
Exif.Image.Model = Canon PowerShot A70
Exif.Image.Orientation = 1
Exif.Image.XResolution = 180/1
Exif.Image.YResolution = 180/1
Exif.Image.ResolutionUnit = 2
Exif.Image.DateTime = 2003:06:21 23:29:18
Exif.Image.YCbCrPositioning = 1
Exif.Image.ExifTag = 196
Exif.Photo.ExposureTime = 1/60
Exif.Photo.FNumber = 40/10
Exif.Photo.ExifVersion = 48 50 50 48
Exif.Photo.DateTimeOriginal = 2003:06:21
23:29:18
Exif.Photo.DateTimeDigitized = 2003:06:21
23:29:18
Exif.Photo.ComponentsConfiguration = 1 2 3 0
Exif.Photo.CompressedBitsPerPixel = 3/1
Exif.Photo.ShutterSpeedValue = 189/32
Exif.Photo.ApertureValue = 128/32
Exif.Photo.ExposureBiasValue = 0/3
Exif.Photo.MaxApertureValue = 128/32
Exif.Photo.MeteringMode = 5
Exif.Photo.Flash = 89
Exif.Photo.FocalLength = 362/32
Exif.Photo.UserComment = ################
##
##
##
##
##
##############################
Exif.Photo.FlashpixVersion = 48 49 48 48

33   Exif.Photo.ColorSpace = 1
Exif.Photo.PixelXDimension = 2048
Exif.Photo.PixelYDimension = 1536
Exif.Photo.InteroperabilityTag = 1540
Exif.Photo.FocalPlaneXResolution = 2048000/208
Exif.Photo.FocalPlaneYResolution = 1536000/156
Exif.Photo.FocalPlaneResolutionUnit = 2
Exif.Photo.SensingMethod = 2
Exif.Photo.FileSource = 3
Exif.Photo.CustomRendered = 0
Exif.Photo.ExposureMode = 0
Exif.Photo.WhiteBalance = 0
Exif.Photo.DigitalZoomRatio = 2048/2048
Exif.Photo.SceneCaptureType = 0
Exif.Iop.InteroperabilityIndex = R98
Exif.Iop.InteroperabilityVersion = 48 49 48 48
Exif.Iop.RelatedImageWidth = 2048
Exif.Iop.RelatedImageLength = 1536
Exif.Thumbnail.Compression = 6
Exif.Thumbnail.XResolution = 180/1
Exif.Thumbnail.YResolution = 180/1
Exif.Thumbnail.ResolutionUnit = 2
Exif.Thumbnail.JPEGInterchangeFormat = 0
Exif.Thumbnail.JPEGInterchangeFormatLength = 5274
Exif.Canon.0x0002 = 2 362 213 159
Exif.Canon.0x0003 = 0 1024 0 0
Exif.Canon.0x0000 = 0 0 0 0 0
Exif.Canon.0x0000 = 0 0 0 0 0
Exif.Canon.0x0013 = 0 0 0 0
Exif.Canon.ImageType = IMG:PowerShot A70 JPEG
Exif.Canon.FirmwareVersion = Firmware Version 1.00
Exif.Canon.ImageNumber = 1010116
Exif.Canon.OwnerName =
Exif.Canon.0x0010 = 19202048
Exif.Canon.0x000d = 68 9 261 261 261 261 261 261 261 261 261 69 0 0 0 0 10 65504 65488 0 882 396 36 80 1034 1205 0 0 0 0 102 0 114
Exif.CanonCs.Macro = 2
Exif.CanonCs.Selftimer = 0
Exif.CanonCs.Quality = 3
Exif.CanonCs.FlashMode = 5
Exif.CanonCs.DriveMode = 0
Exif.CanonCs.0x0006 = 0

Exif.CanonCs.FocusMode = 4
Exif.CanonCs.0x0008 = 0
Exif.CanonCs.0x0009 = 1
Exif.CanonCs.ImageSize = 0
Exif.CanonCs.EasyMode = 0
Exif.CanonCs.DigitalZoom = 0
Exif.CanonCs.Contrast = 0
Exif.CanonCs.Saturation = 0
Exif.CanonCs.Sharpness = 0
Exif.CanonCs.ISOSpeed = 15
Exif.CanonCs.MeteringMode = 3
Exif.CanonCs.FocusType = 1
Exif.CanonCs.AFPoint = 16385
Exif.CanonCs.ExposureProgram = 0
Exif.CanonCs.0x0015 = 65535
Exif.CanonCs.0x0016 = 65535
Exif.CanonCs.Lens = 519 173 32
Exif.CanonCs.0x001a = 129
Exif.CanonCs.0x001b = 192
Exif.CanonCs.FlashActivity = 1
Exif.CanonCs.FlashDetails = 8200
Exif.CanonCs.0x001e = 0
Exif.CanonCs.0x001f = 0
Exif.CanonCs.FocusContinuous = 0
Exif.CanonCs.AESetting = 0
Exif.CanonCs.ImageStabilization = 65535
Exif.CanonCs.DisplayAperture = 0
Exif.CanonCs.ZoomSourceWidth = 2048
Exif.CanonCs.ZoomTargetWidth = 2048
Exif.CanonCs.0x0026 = 0
Exif.CanonCs.0x0027 = 1
Exif.CanonCs.PhotoEffect = 0
Exif.CanonCs.0x0029 = 0
Exif.CanonCs.ColorTone = 32767
Exif.CanonCs.0x002b = 0
Exif.CanonCs.0x002c = 0
Exif.CanonCs.0x002d = 0
Exif.CanonPi.0x0001 = 5
Exif.CanonPi.ImageWidth = 2048
Exif.CanonPi.ImageHeight = 1536
Exif.CanonPi.ImageWidthAsShot = 2048
Exif.CanonPi.ImageHeightAsShot = 256
Exif.CanonPi.0x0006 = 369
Exif.CanonPi.0x0007 = 42
Exif.CanonPi.0x0008 = 0
Exif.CanonPi.0x0009 = 65166

Exif.CanonPi.0x000a = 0
Exif.CanonPi.0x000b = 370
Exif.CanonPi.0x000c = 0
Exif.CanonPi.0x000d = 65488
Exif.CanonPi.0x000e = 0
Exif.CanonPi.0x000f = 0
Exif.CanonPi.0x0010 = 0
Exif.CanonPi.0x0011 = 48
Exif.CanonPi.0x0012 = 0
Exif.CanonPi.0x0013 = 0
Exif.CanonSi.0x0001 = 48
Exif.CanonSi.ISOSpeed = 128
Exif.CanonSi.0x0003 = 65255
Exif.CanonSi.TargetAperture = 128

COLOPHON

Real Irish Fairies of Donegal was written and designed by J.A. Greenleaf on a MacBook Pro, using Adobe InDesign, CS6, and is set in Minion Pro typeface. Published by Swordpoint Intercontinental, Ltd., La Vista, Nebraska, USA, and distributed throughout the world through fine bookshops, and online through Amazon.com, Amazon.ca, Amazon.co.uk, Amazon.fr, Amazon.de and other online booksellers.

If you cannot find a copy in your local bookstore, please request they special order. If they cannot, you can order directly from the Publisher, using the following order forms. Simply photocopy the appropriate order form (US$, euro or sterling) and mail to the address on the order form. Payment is accepted in US dollars, euro and British pounds sterling.

You can also order via the author's website, www.jagreenleaf.com. Payment by all major credit cards as well as PayPal.

All books ordered from the publisher will be hand-signed by the author!

$ Book Order Form

Swordpoint Intercontinental, Ltd.
7202 Giles Road, Suite 4212
La Vista, NE 68128 USA

Buyer: _____   Date: _____ 201____
Address: _____
City: _____ State: _____
Zip: _____
Phone: (____)_____
Email: _____@_____.com

Billing address: [   ] (check if same as above, otherewise, enter billing address below:

Address: _____
City: _____State: _____
Zip: _____

ORDER

Item	Quantity	Price	Total
Real Irish Fairies book		$12.99 each	$
(signed by author)			
Shipping, USA		$5.00 each	$
7% NE tax, if applicable			
		Sale total:	$

Payment: (do not send cash)

[ ] Check (Payable to Swordpoint Intercontinental, Ltd.)

[ ] Money order (Payable to Swordpoint Intercontinental, Ltd.)

[ ] Credit card (enter details below)

Name on credit card: _____
Number: _____
Expiration date: _____/20____
3-digit number on revers (Visa/MC), 4-digits on front (Amex) _____

€ Book Order Form

Joseph A. Greenleaf
"Solas Tobann"
Ballyhillion
Malin Head
Co Donegal, Ireland

Buyer: _____   Date: _____201___
Address: _____
City: _____ County_____
Post code: _____
Country: _____
Phone: (____)_____
Email: _____@_____._____

Billing address: [ ] (check if same as above, otherwise, enter billing address below:

Address: _____
City: _____County_____
Post code: _____
Country: _____

ORDER

Item	Quantity	Price	Total
Real Irish Fairies book		€9.99 each	€
(signed by author)			
Shipping, Europe		€5.00 each	€
		Nil VAT for books	###################
		Sale total:	€

Payment: (do not send cash)

[ ] Cheque (Payable to Joseph A. Greenleaf) [Shipment may be delayed until cheque clears]

[ ] Postal/bank order (Payable to Joseph A. Greenleaf)

[ ] Credit card (enter details below)

Name on credit card: _____
Number: _____
Issue Date: _____/20____   Expiration date: _____/20____
3-digit number on revers (Visa/MC), 4-digits on front (Amex) _____

£ Book Order Form

Joseph A. Greenleaf
"Solas Tobann"
Ballyhillion
Malin Head
Co Donegal, Ireland

Buyer: _____ Date: _____201___
Address: _____
City: _____ County_____
Post code: _____ United Kingdom
Phone: (____)_____
Email: _____@_____._____

Billing address: [   ] (check if same as above, otherwise, enter billing address below:

Address: _____
City: _____County_____
Post code: _____ United Kingdom

ORDER

Item	Quantity	Price	Total
Real Irish Fairies book		£9.99 each	£
(signed by author)			
Shipping, UK		£5.00 each	£
		Nil VAT for books	###################
		Sale total:	£

Payment: (do not send cash)

[ ] Cheque (Payable to Joseph A. Greenleaf) [Shipment may be delayed until cheque clears]

[ ] Postal/bank order (Payable to Joseph A. Greenleaf)

[ ] Credit card (enter details below)

Name on credit card: _____

Number: _____

Issue Date: _____/20____   Expiration date: _____/20____

3-digit number on revers (Visa/MC), 4-digits on front (Amex) _____

COTTINGLEY FAIRIES

No book of real fairies is complete without reproducing the most famous *fake* fairy photographs in history, the Cottingley Fairies. In 1917, two cousins in England, using one of girl's father's camera, took photographs of paper dolls and represented them as fairy photographs. Sir Author Conan Doyle, the author of the Sherlock Holmes mysteries, was quite a bit more gullible than Sherlock would have been. He proclaimed them to be genuine, and even wrote a book about them. (In one of the photographs, Elsie has her right hand extended. She could have been a great pianist, as her fingers are twice as long as a normal human's! Sir Arthur didn't notice that, apparently.)

It was not until the 1980s that the two cousins admitted that they had faked the photographs, although they contended the fifth one was real.

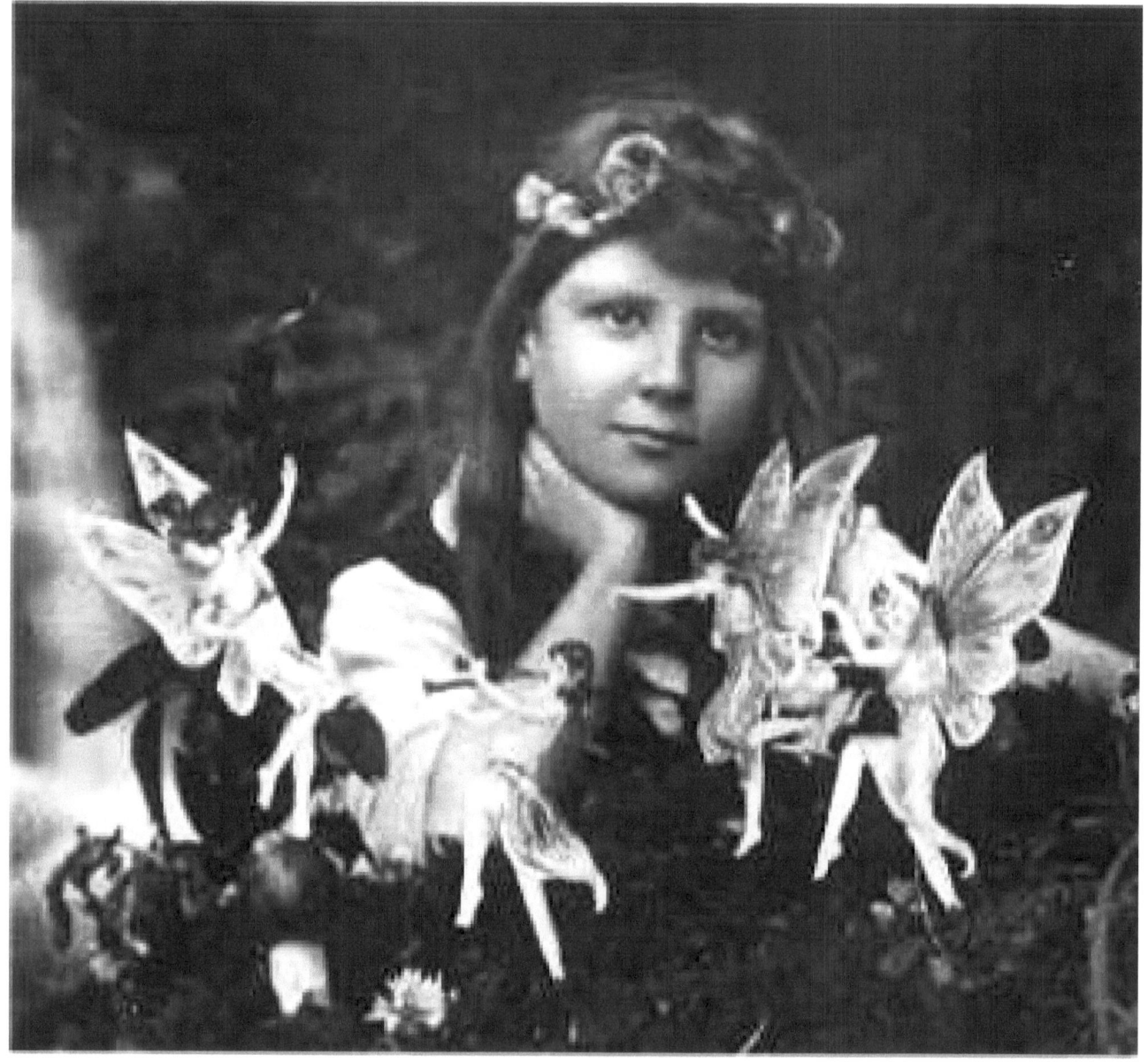

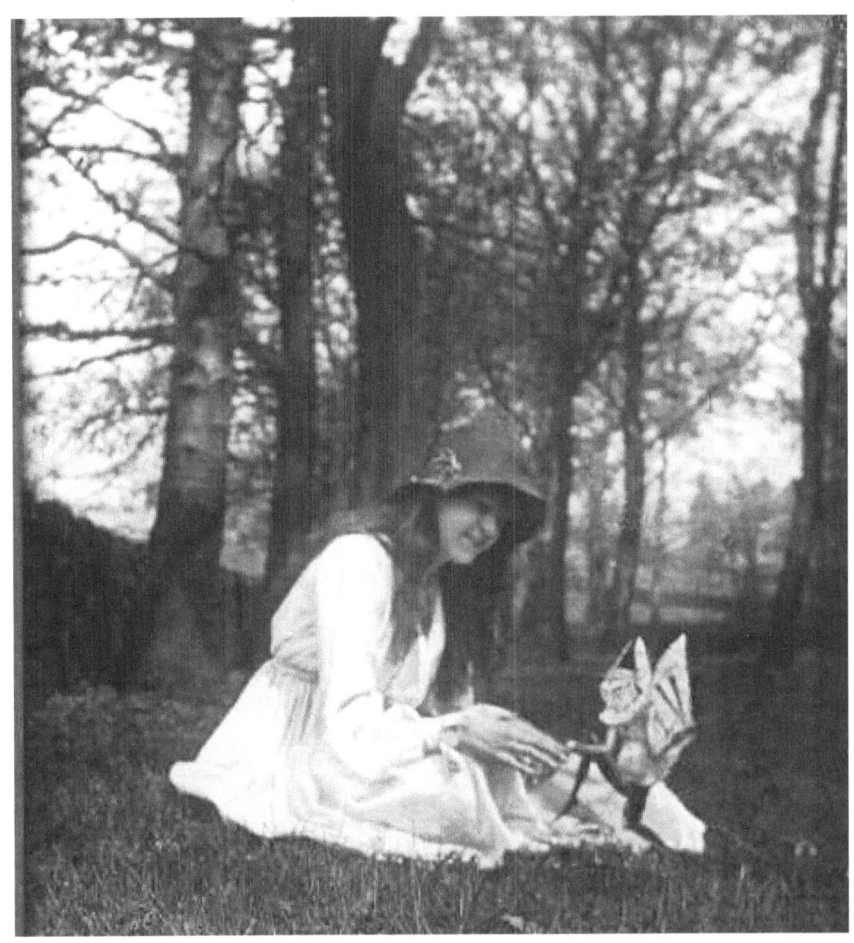

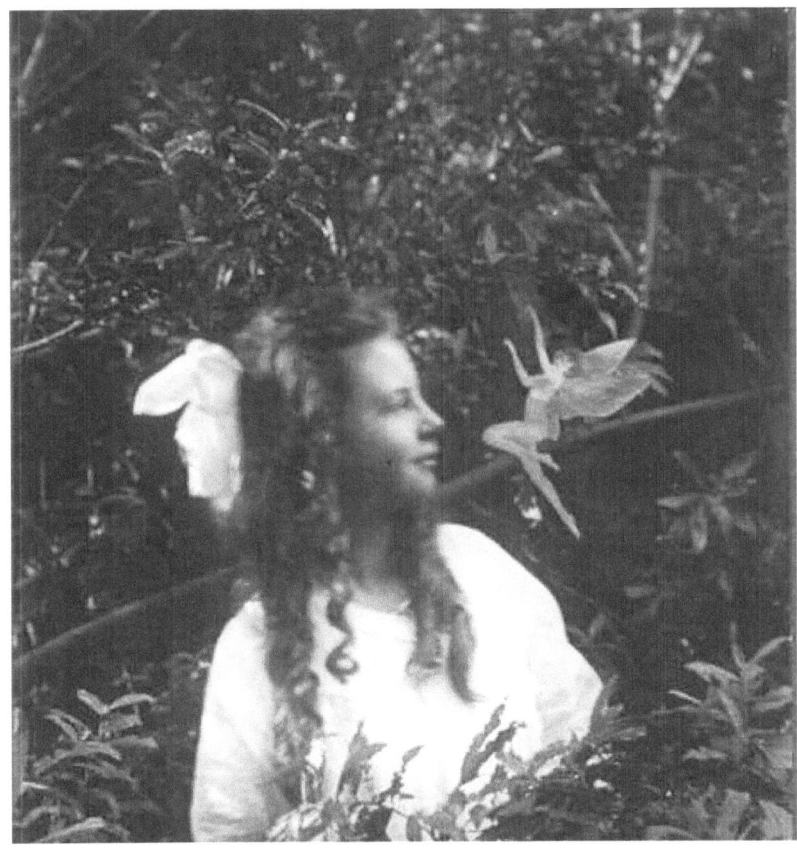

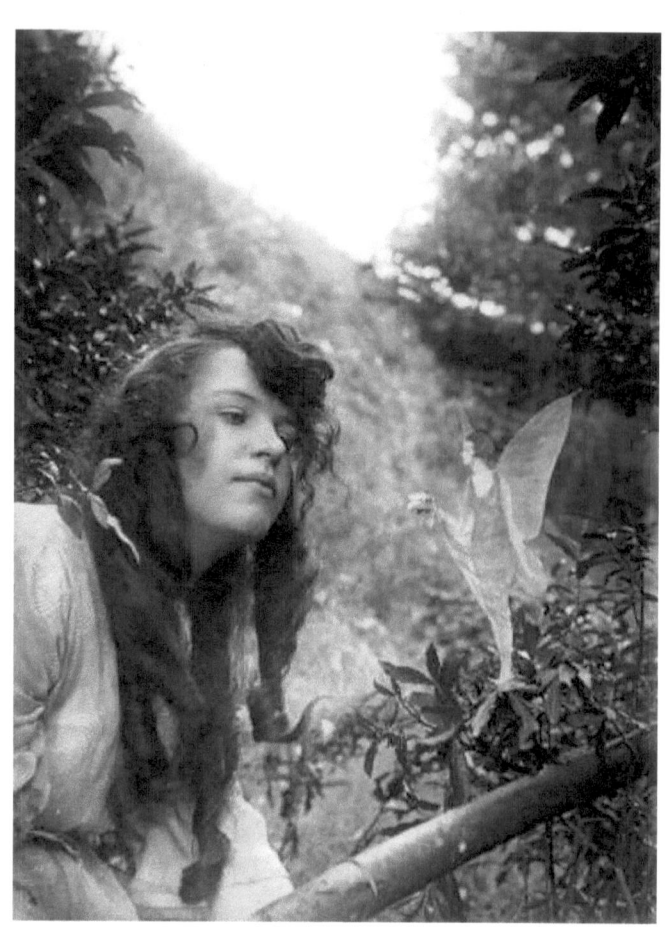

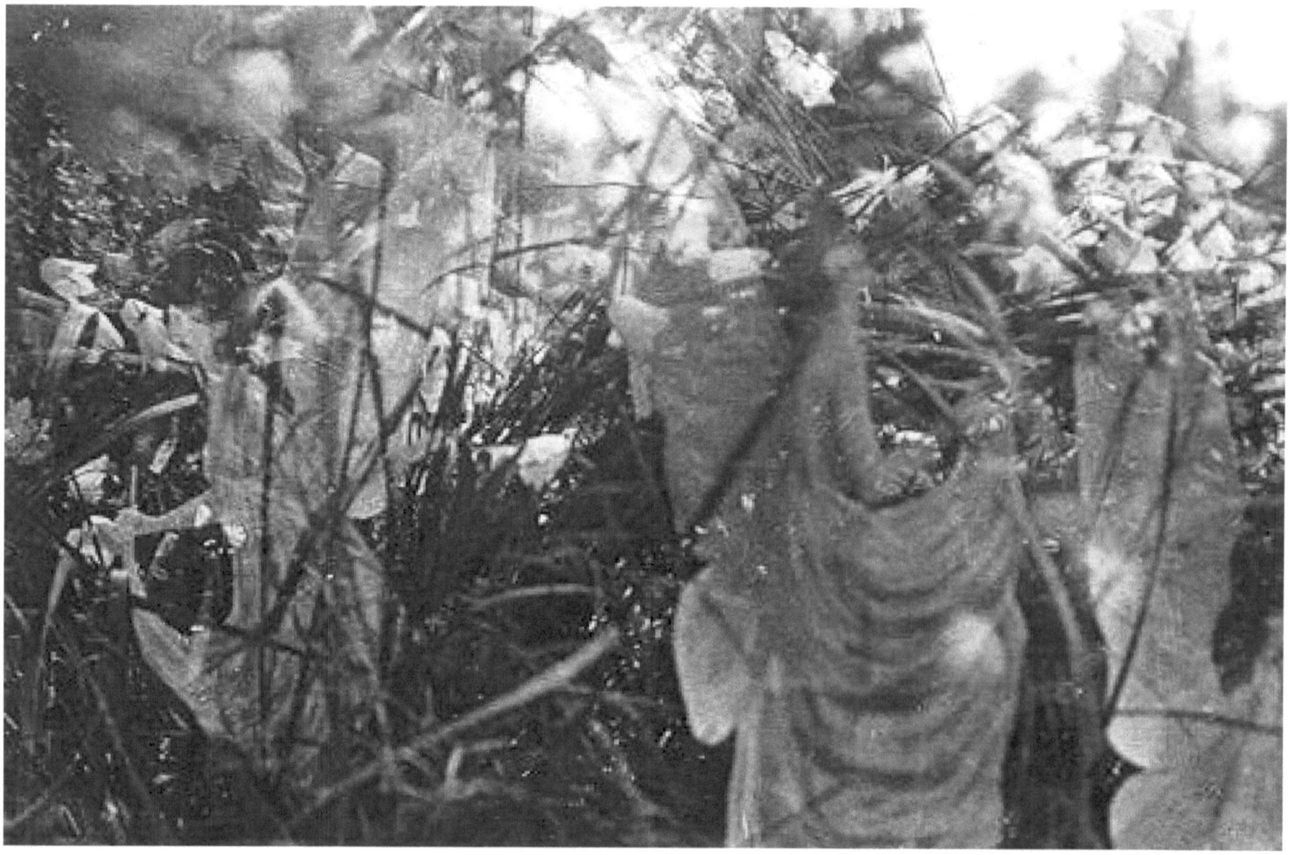

www.ingramcontent.com/pod-product-compliance
Lightning Source LLC
Chambersburg PA
CBHW051059180526
45172CB00002B/696